Betsy Kerekes is both comical and compelling as she takes a clear-eyed yet light-hearted look at the challenges of raising a Catholic family in today's secular world. Just the book for a frazzled parent!
— Dr. John Bergsma, Ph.D. Professor of Theology,
Franciscan University of Steubenville

Through her engaging, conversational style, Betsy Kerekes presents parents with the means for a happier, more mindful parenting experience, and provides quite a few laughs in the process. A great read for both new and experienced parents.
— Dr. Gregory Bottaro, Founder and Director of the
CatholicPsych Institute, author of *The Mindful Catholic:
Finding God One Moment at a Time*

The endorsement for this book could be summed up in one acronym: ROFL! Get it. Read it out loud. Then laugh out loud over lines like this: "How best to handle tears and whining can be summed up in one word: Oreos."
— Jennifer Roback Morse, Ph.D., Founder and President
of The Ruth Institute

Betsy Kerekes combines a TED Talk's worth of wisdom with enough humor to bring down the house at a comedy club. A generous measure of compassion and prayer round out this encouraging manual for moms who despair of ever having it all together.
— Barb Szyszkiewicz, editor, CatholicMom.com

Witty, insightful, and full of practical advice, Betsy Kerekes shows how almost any difficult parenting situation can be handled better with humor. *Be a Happier Parent or Laugh Trying* imparts solid parenting wisdom with a whimsical approach and a thoroughly Catholic perspective. With this light-hearted slant on the most serious of topics, you'll learn to parent with confidence while

keeping your sanity and getting your kids to heaven.
— Marc Cardaronella, author of *Keep Your Kids Catholic: Sharing Your Faith and Making It Stick*

This is a refreshing and hilarious book, chock-full of wisdom and laugh-out-loud stories from the parenting trenches. A fun and encouraging read.
— Catherine Harmon, Managing Editor, Catholic World Report

Who doesn't want a happier, more fulfilling parenting experience? This book will help you attain that dream. It's easy to read, witty, entertaining, and full of real-life stories and parenting advice that will help guide you and your whole family to greater happiness and unity.
— Bryan Mercier, Catholic speaker, apologist, and author of *Why Do You Believe in GOD?*

Be a Happier Parent or Laugh Trying

Betsy Kerekes

Our
Sunday
Visitor

www.osv.com
Our Sunday Visitor Publishing Division
Our Sunday Visitor, Inc.
Huntington, Indiana 46750

Our Sunday Visitor Publishing Division
Our Sunday Visitor, Inc.
200 Noll Plaza
Huntington, IN 46750
1-800-348-2440

ISBN: 978-1-68192-292-8 (Inventory No. T1969)
eISBN: 978-1-68192-293-5
LCCN: 2019930128

Cover and interior design: Lindsey Riesen
Cover art: Shutterstock.com

PRINTED IN THE UNITED STATES OF AMERICA

Dedication

To Our Lady, the Blessed Mother of Jesus, our greatest model for one of the most difficult jobs of all.

A sacrifice to be real must cost, must hurt, must empty ourselves. … The fruit of love is service, the fruit of service is peace.

• SAINT TERESA OF CALCUTTA •

(And peace in one's home means happiness.)

Table of Contents

INTRODUCTION

I have three daughters: ages twelve, ten, and seven. After having them in my care for so many years, I feel it safe to say that they are, in a word, awesome. For the most part, they're obedient, helpful, and kind; they can feed, clothe, and bathe themselves, and they change the toilet paper rolls. In other words, they can fend for themselves while Mom sleeps in. My life for several years was easy.

Perhaps a little too easy.

So God decided I needed a shake-up.

Enter Baby Boy.

After no live births in seven years, I naturally began to assume that part of my life was over, and so I did the unthinkable: I started getting rid of the baby gear. And of course, blammo! Baby! Whether this is the start of a second wave of children or just my encore performance remains to be seen.

When people found out I was having my first boy, there was great rejoicing in the land. Everyone — friends, family, the librarian, the cashier at Food 4 Less, the sample lady at Costco, and pretty much every nurse while I was in labor — gave me the lowdown on boys, and let me tell you, each 100 percent guaranteed statement contradicted the last. Either this child is assured to be the easiest ever, or a little terror. I have yet to find out. He's too young to roll over, let alone either burn down small villages or convert the residents to Christianity, so we still await his grand purpose in life. Though, kicking my husband in the face when he kissed my pregnant belly might not have been a good sign.

I always did want a priest in the family, so each time I rejoiced "Yes! Another girl!" my loving husband reminded me that "You can't have a priest in the family, if you don't have any boys." So, Baby Boy is my shot. But for now, I'm back to the days of wondering why onesie designers make the top halves so much dirtier than the halves that hide under the pants.

I won't spend much time talking about babies in this book. Lord knows you've already received advice on the matter from everyone and their cousin's half-sister's babysitter's free-range chicken inspector. The usual advice is to sleep when the baby sleeps, which is fine and well so long as that's your only child. Other advice for newborns is more in-depth, and a myriad of books on the topic will let you know how many naps are normal at a particular age and warn you that babies sometimes go days without soiling a diaper. What they don't tell you is when baby finally does go, you'll need a hazmat suit.

Motherhood has taught me a few things about babies that books can't. For instance, if you want a crawling baby (or toddler, for that matter) to come to you, pretend to hide. Then peek around the wall or couch and gasp when you're spotted. He'll come as fast as his little arms and legs will allow.

Another discovery is that babies — like dogs and honeybees — sense fear. When I've tried to get mine to sleep and am all stressed out, as in, "Go to sleep, already! Please!" their little eyes stay wide open. On the other hand, if I'm sitting there spacing out, picturing my dream home, the kid falls asleep before I know it. Suddenly I'm like, "Oh, hello there, sleeping Baby Boy. When did you get here?" Try it sometime. If not the dream home, I recommend the dream vacation. Perfectly acceptable for it to not include Baby. No judgment.

I firmly believe there are as many different ways to parent as there are parents. You do what works for you, and don't worry what everyone else thinks. And especially do not compare your child to others. A mom who had a baby around the same time as I had my first made a comment about teething. I mentioned that my daughter had four teeth coming in at once, only because I thought it unusual. The other mom seemed upset by this news and got defensive — over teeth — as though the rate at which children sprout teeth somehow determines who will go to a community college and who will go to Harvard.

And so I learned early that it's best to resist the urge to talk baby with other parents. The comparing seems endless. Don't worry how other babies measure up. This is a key to happy parenting, as is learning to let go and laugh even when the household chaos or calamities make you want to cry. Crying is still an option, but isn't laughing more fun? When in doubt, laugh it out.

From one parent in the trenches to another, we've all been there. Parenting is hard, but it doesn't have to be a burden. Why? Because parenting can also be a blast. I hope the tricks of the trade I've learned along the way and am sharing with you, will help you be a happier parent by making the job easier. If you can discipline effectively, you'll have fewer tantrums to deal with. If you can teach your kids to pick up after themselves and do chores, that's less cleaning for you, and a more peaceful, organized home. If you can wrangle them at church and instill in them a lasting faith, getting them to heaven will be that much more successful. And furthermore, the less time you need to spend parenting, the more time you have to enjoy having fun with your kids. All around, having fun with your kids makes you a happier parent.

And you being their parent, well, you wouldn't have it any other way.

Enjoy!

CHAPTER ONE

Being a Happy Parent

"True holiness consists in doing God's
will with a smile."

• SAINT TERESA OF CALCUTTA •

For most people, parenthood begins with an infant, and that's sort of a raw deal. Sure, they're cute and cuddly and they can't dump all your Tupperware on the kitchen floor yet, or unravel an entire roll of toilet paper into the toilet, but they're still difficult. I know because I currently have one. Or rather, we have one. I made the mistake of referring to him as "my baby" within earshot of my seven-year-old. "He's not *your* baby, Mom. He's *our* baby, too." I stand corrected.

So when *our* baby was overdue, my fellow mom-friends felt so much sympathy for me. I, on the other hand, relished how easy he was to take care of while still inside of me. All his needs were being met, no poopy diapers had to be changed, and I could cart him everywhere with my hands free. He was like a Bluetooth baby.

Now things are more difficult — and I know difficult. I've earned two PhDs and three masters, completed both a decathlon and a triathlon, was CEO of a Fortune 500 company, swam the English Channel, rode a barrel over Niagara Falls, and flew on the Apollo 13 Mission. (I wasn't in the movie because I accidentally insulted Kevin Bacon's mother.) Despite having totally, totally done all those things, I find parenting is still the hardest job ever. And the most rewarding.

During a homily at Mass, the deacon said, "Think about how God loves you," and so I did. Almost immediately the image of my baby boy popped into my mind and my heart swelled with love. This is how God the Father loves us, his children, despite how frustrating we can be. Baby Joseph doesn't listen to — or do — what I say, cries inexplicably, and gets bored easily even when he's given lots of shiny new toys to play with. Sound familiar? Joseph has no idea all I do for him and the sacrifices I make. God's like, "Yeah. I might know a thing or two about that." Yet, I love my child completely and unequivocally, like my heavenly father loves me. (Baby Joe is also astonishingly cute, so there's another similarity.)

Being a happy parent means focusing on the love we feel for our children, not on how trying and tiring they can be. It's taking an attitude of "the milk bottle is half full" rather than "that bottle is half empty and gosh I'd better refill it soon before he starts shrieking." (But go ahead and refill now, because shrieking babies are no fun.) Recalling the joy children bring us is the antidote to the frustration they also bring. My mom frequently says to my dad, "It's a good thing you're so cute." I find myself doing the same with Joe.

Once, when my husband was holding Joe, I came walking down the hallway toward him. When he saw me, his face lit up and his arms and legs started jerking around like crazy. I'm going to hold on to that image forever, especially when he's seventeen, or if he ever eats the last of the ice cream. I also appreciate that he's not bothered by my appearance in the morning, or any other time of day for that matter. This is the joy a happy parent must recall.

Focusing on the blessings in your life, even if your house is a mess or the laundry is piling up, is the antidote to the parenting pits. Clearly your kids don't mind those messes since they enjoy making them, and rolling around in a pile of unfolded laundry is the rainy-day equivalent of jumping in a pile of leaves. Why deprive your children of that joy? Instead, maintain an attitude of gratitude by focusing on the positive. Your children have enough clothes that they can get some dirty. The dishes stacked in the sink prove that you have ample food for your family. You have this wonderful book in your hands. Ice cream exists. And the list goes on and on.

Granted, during the sleep-deprived newborn days, it's hard to stay positive. We know God doesn't give us more than we can handle, but sometimes I feel like he gives me too much credit, as in, "I'm flattered you think I can do all of this, but I respectfully disagree." To combat that sentiment, I choose to latch on to the sweet little things while they last. For instance, there's nothing quite like waking up in the morning next to my baby, both of us lying on our backs, moving our limbs and grunting: me because I'm stretching, him because he's filling his diaper. The next step is starting the day with a prayer, even if you mean to say, "Help me know and follow your will today," but instead it comes out as, "Just five more minutes," or "Please tell me I remembered to set the coffeemaker last night." If I can read just a snippet of something holy, such as the life of a saint, I find it inspires me and provides a little more patience to make it through the day.

Patience does seem to be the key, though often it feels like I've tucked that key in my back pocket, forgetting there's a hole in it. For the short while that I'm able to keep my patience, it's quite helpful. At other times, I try not to sigh too heavily. I don't just mean patience with your children — obviously that — but patience with yourself and your spouse, too. Along with that comes recognizing that you'll make mistakes. When I think back on the ones I've made with my children, it makes me cringe, sometimes even cry. It's a good thing they have memories as short as their attention spans. It also helps knowing that I'm not the only parent who messes up. I saw a picture of a T-shirt tag that bore the instructions: "Remove child before washing." I mean, if that has to be stated for some parents, I can't be doing too badly.

It's a good thing we can learn from our mistakes. "The lesson retain, but forget the pain," is a good motto. Once when we were staying at my in-laws, my young daughter was napping in the basement. The rest of us were sitting on the front lawn. The thought occurred to me that she would be waking up soon and I should check on her, but I didn't feel like getting up. Soon she came out, crying, with my sister-in-law who'd heard her. She woke up in a strange place and didn't know how to find me. After roughly a decade, that incident still gets me. I've learned that when you have a thought like, "Go check on your kid," it's likely your guardian angel or the Holy Spirit prompting you to action. I ignored it. He probably tried not to sigh too heavily. Thankfully, children are amazingly resilient. Even when you screw up, they have a tendency to overlook your shortcomings and love you anyway. We can learn a lot from our children.

Letting go can be a tough skill to learn, but taking a deep breath and moving on after an unfortunate incident will help you maintain a happier demeanor, especially when it comes to things you have no control over. Some days your children are just going to be fussy, like they're taking turns or have it scheduled on a secret calendar. Keeping a sense of humor helps. Once I asked a friend how her kids were. She responded: "For sale."

If you're a perfectionist, having children may be particularly difficult, especially if you're the type who tries to maintain a spotless home and the aforementioned laundry leaping idea doesn't do it for you. You can be happier if you adopt this principle: let it go. Embroider it on a pillow if necessary.

Here's a scenario: after breakfast, the floor under your table looks like the leftovers at the carnival in *Charlotte's Web*. You want to sweep it immediately, but you're unable because you're wrangling tiny people all day. Lunch happens, and now the floor looks like the streets of New Orleans after Mardi Gras. You want to pull your hair out, but you still haven't found time to clean. The solution? Make like Elsa and let it go. I don't mean go a week without sweeping under the table. If mice move in to clean up the mess for you, well, that could be a win or a loss. The floor is getting cleaned, but if those mice start building temples to their gods complete with statues made from food scraps that impressively resemble your children, then you may have a problem. Get out the broom and destroy a civilization. But for those everyday things that put the perfectionist in you on high alert, remember that the world won't end and your house won't fall down around you if you don't get to it right away. Take a deep breath, relax a little. Have another cup of coffee. The floor can wait.

Eventually you'll reach the point where you *are* able to get some cleaning or other important tasks completed. For me, accomplishing a long-overdue task is priceless, much like a gemstone due to its rareness. Someone also told me you get endorphins from crossing things off your to-do list, which is why I have "Cross something off to-do list" written several times on mine.

If you take care of business right away, you get that sense of fulfillment and keep the task off a growing to-do list. Instead of staring at the cobweb in the corner for days, thinking, "I should take care of that," just take care of it. But since dropping everything to climb onto the desk with a partially used napkin isn't always feasible, take a moment to think of the one thing that most needs to get done. Make that your objective for the day. Dusting the whole house? Ugh! Dust just the living room? Okay. That I can do. So far, my family hasn't minded that the vacuum moves from room to room each day as I tackle the carpets piecemeal. If I can just do one chore outside of the standard must-do-for-survival a day, I feel productive, which makes me happy. So today, scrub a toilet, dust just the living room, vacuum only the hallway, or finally put away that one thing that's been sitting on the counter for weeks. I for one, after staring at the chipped paint on the windowsill for a month, am going to suck it up, sit myself down, and finally write my husband a note to patch it.

There are rare — okay, occasional — on second thought, frequent times where I haven't followed my own advice and the dust gets to the point where the girls are drawing in it. (I like to do my part to support the arts.) This reminds me that it's time to host a game night. That's how I trick myself and the kids into cleaning. They love game nights because I let them stay up a smidge longer, and they also get to try all the tasty treats. They probably further appreciate that, busily engaged in conversation with a guest, I'll typically say yes to them having just one more whatever that I would not allow under normal circumstances. The house gets clean, which makes me happy. The kids help, happier still. They get to stay up and eat yum-yums — a win for them. And my husband and I? We get to spend time with friends, another key to happiness. Although some nights I'm tired and regret the decision to have a party, as soon as people arrive, I perk up. Even though I'm an introvert, social time is great for the psyche. That reminds me. Let me check the dust level. Yep, it's time to send another e-vite.

The other great thing about hosting game nights is it's a date where you don't have to hire a babysitter. I'm sure you've heard that you still need to date your spouse post-wedding to keep your relationship strong. Maintaining that marital strength adds to your happiness as a parent, also. Not only does an intact marriage make you happier, studies have shown that when parents are happy, their kids are happier, too. Having a spouse who is, hopefully, your best friend, means you can help each other through the inevitable tough times of parenting. During these rough patches, sometimes your only recourse besides each other is acceptance with joy. (And if joy isn't around, acceptance with your other friend, chocolate.)

A friend's son gives her the hardest time at bedtime if he so much as takes a five-minute nap during the day. She tries to keep him from falling asleep, but sometimes it happens in the car while she's driving. She's done everything but squirt him with a water bottle — like you do when your cat jumps on the counter. She hates the struggle that even this tiny nap will bring in the evening. There's no way to fix her circumstances, so all that's left is an attitude adjustment. Anticipating and accepting the difficulty makes it less frustrating.

Another example is when we took Joe on a "vacation" when he was five months old. I have since learned my lesson. It was awful. When I could get him to sleep, he only stayed asleep for thirty minutes. That was for naps *and* at nighttime. I was miserable. He was miserable. Everyone in a five-mile radius was miserable. Finally, I decided to just accept it. I chose to be prepared for, rather than irritated by, the short sleep. My attitude was the only thing I had the power to change. In doing so, I was able to relax my expectations and be happier by making the most of the trip, despite Joe's less-than-ideal sleep habits. And now I know for next time to bring one of those noise machines that mimic the ocean, rain forest, or New York City traffic complete with honking horns and people yelling, "Hey, I'm walkin' here!"

The other key to riding out calamity is remaining calm. A priest told a story about the car breaking down while his mom was driving him to school. She called her husband to come bail them out. It was inconvenient to be pulled away from work, and annoying to then get him to school so late, but if his parents were irritated, you would never have known. There was nothing they could do other than fix the situation and be on their way. Complaining about the dumb old car wouldn't help anything, so why bother? When you can't change something that's happening to you, what's the use in letting it drive you crazy? Staying calm in a negative situation makes one happier, or at least less unhappy.

Remaining calm sets a better example than we realize. Imagine you're potty training your child. (Did you just shudder? My apologies.) Now imagine you take your child to the potty, but he doesn't want to go. You try again later and still nothing. You ask him if he needs to go. He insists he doesn't. Next thing you know, his pants are wet. You, frustrated by the whole experience, kind of lose it. "Look what you did! You wet your pants! I tried to get you to go on the potty. I sat you down, you said you didn't need to go. Then I asked again, and you still said no. One minute later you've wet yourself. Now I have to wash you up and find clean clothes and—" you know the rest. Unbeknownst to you, this reaction is teaching your child to lie in order to avoid seeing you angry or be yelled at. Express disappointment, sure, but remain calm and patient. You want your child to feel safe coming to you with the truth when she ran a purple marker across the back of the white couch or when he threw a ball indoors and knocked over a lamp. If such incidents happen and you fly off the handle, don't be surprised when you're met with tight lips after asking who swirled a magnet across the computer screen.

Besides, such incidents are part of parenting and are to be expected. If your kids empty the contents of a flour bag all over the kitchen, or dump every single jigsaw puzzle you own into a single pile (both of these happened to friends of mine), take photos for social media and bask in the sympathy. And the laughter. Just remember to share the story at this child's wedding reception.

Not all messes are that calamitous, but they're bound to occur regardless, so look on the bright side. Your children played in the mud and got filthy. They were being creative, getting exercise, and having fun while you got some quiet time. Children and their messes can be cleaned. Things that break can be repaired or replaced. Baby teeth fall out anyway, so who cares if you forgot to brush them tonight? Same goes for eating healthy. You can load them up with vegetables tomorrow. They will eventually potty train, be able to feed themselves, get dressed by themselves, and more. There are pros and cons at every age. Focus on the pros.

You might think you'll be truly happy if you could just have a girl, a boy, your dream home, a new car, a better job, or an ice cream shop to open up within walking distance. Perhaps you feel you'll be happier when the kids are older and easier, or when they're no longer teenagers, or when you have an empty nest, or when you can finally retire. But if you continue thinking that way — waiting for that next thing that you're sure will make you happy — you'll never be happy. Instead, find the joy in your life as a parent today.

CHAPTER TWO

Being a Good Parent

"Never be in a hurry; do everything quietly
and in a calm spirit. Do not lose your inner peace
for anything whatsoever, even if your whole
world seems upset."

• SAINT FRANCIS DE SALES •

Having read the above quote, I know one thing for certain: Saint Francis was never on a conference call when he spotted his potty-training daughter about to wipe poo off her underwear with the dish cleaning rag. His point as it applies to parenting, however, is that to be a good parent we must set the right example by our attitude and demeanor.

We can't go wrong imitating people like Alice of Montbar. She had seven children, six of whom have been beatified, and the seventh is Saint Bernard of Clairvaux. She married the chief advisor to a French duke. That meant they could live large, but Alice wasn't down with that. Based on their station in life, they could, and by the social standards of the day, should, eat sumptuously at every meal, but Alice kept things simple. They also dressed more plainly than was standard for their rank. Back in the eleventh century, Alice was the first to say, "Modest is hottest," but in French. You can quote me on that, though I wouldn't recommend it since I totally just made that up. Most scandalous of all was her propensity to go out and feed the hungry and tend to the sick in a way that would've made Saint Teresa of Calcutta proud. Based on how holy her kids turned out, I'm pretty sure she took her children with her, teaching them without words to be humble and to care for those less fortunate.

In our day this might translate to having food on hand for homeless people on street corners, giving to your parish food pantry, or visiting the elderly in nursing homes. When I was a child, my mom would bake cakes and bring them to the local nursing home to celebrate all the residents with birthdays that month. The employees kindly hung a sign with those residents' names so we could sing to them accordingly. Of course, not all the birthday celebrants would attend. It was usually just the same old faces (excuse the pun) each time, but that day was probably a highlight of their month. The elderly love seeing children and having visitors. Bringing cake helps. I don't remember there being ice cream. I probably ate it in the car on the way.

Our children learn a lot from our example and teaching including, of course, manners. I sent my six-year-old to deliver lemons and oranges from our yard to the widow next door. Worried that she might rudely deliver the fruit and leave without a word, I called to her, "Don't forget to say, 'You're welcome.'" When she returned, she gave me the full report: "I rang the doorbell, and when the lady opened the door, I said, 'You're welcome!' and handed her the bag." I guess I should've been more specific.

Sometimes teaching our kids to be specific, and honest, can backfire — though I'm not saying it shouldn't be tried. One day, my youngest daughter said, "These eggs are delicious, Grandma." My mom replied, "Why, thank you!" Then my daughter gave her reasoning: "Because I like things that are burnt."

Parenting requires so much diligence, not to mention energy. A friend says the first step in good parenting is to get up off the couch. How often have you, like me, told a kid to "Come here and tell me" or asked an older child to check on their sibling, because you didn't want to go wherever she was? Or, like another friend, when told a child was injured, responded with, "Is it bleeding?" Now, eight kids in, she calls, "Is it gushing?" Anything less and she can't be bothered. Granted, these kids have more energy in their tiny legs than we have in our whole bodies.

If you are sitting on the couch, however, it's easier to be at your child's eye level. Making eye contact shows you're giving your complete attention — something kids crave. Okay fine, adults too. Too often I'll be typing, still looking at the screen but slightly turning my head in my daughter's direction, saying, "Uh huh" and "Okay" without really hearing what she's saying. Usually it's nothing important (from my perspective), but if I'm not careful, I may find her eating cookies for breakfast (kid after my own heart), with my apparent permission.

Children need our attention for their emotional well-being. A friend with a large family noticed one of her kids had gone quiet for several days. Of course, with adolescents, simply asking what was wrong got this mom nowhere. Then she had the idea to go shopping and invite only this child to accompany her. After their special mommy-daughter time, the girl perked up and was back to her normal self. Whenever the melancholy seemed to creep back in, this mom knew it was time for some one-on-one again. She said to her husband, "Sorry, honey. She *needs* me to take her shopping," as she grabbed her purse and dashed.

What a wonderful experience it is for our children to have mommy or daddy all to themselves to explain what's in their drawing, or describe a bug they found, or — heaven help us — verbally illustrate a dream they had last night. That last one is the worst. That's when I let them follow me to the kitchen so I can at least be scrubbing potatoes while I listen. I find that giving my attention to one kid at a time keeps me from being stressed out by the big picture. When my baby needs me, I take him to his room and shut the door so I can focus just on him. This only works when your other children aren't likely to shave the dog or set the couch on fire. But if I can ignore everything else for just a few minutes, it's incredibly soothing. I can say, "It's just you and me, baby. You have me completely." Of course, looking at his cute, chubby face is always therapeutic.

Extending these principles, you can spend one-on-one time with each child as a way of "checking in" or making sure all is well. I start with a finger and toenail check on baby Joe. All clipped and ready to go. When did I last give him a bath? Shoot, has it been that long? Don't tell my husband. Then I work my way up to the next kid until she goes on for too long about Calvin and Hobbes. Next one: Do you need anything? Order more books from the library? Can do! And the oldest girl — I have to strap in for that one. Once I've completed the rounds, I have peace of mind knowing everyone is present and accounted for (lest I inadvertently lose one), and each one's needs are being met. And if not, I'll do what I can to be sure they are. Pro tip: Do this every once and a while with your spouse, too!

Younger kids might be bothered that they can't do the same things as their older siblings, like check the bear traps or drive the Batmobile. At a playground a little girl was crying because she couldn't swing across the monkey bars like her big brother. The mom assured the girl that her brother was able because he'd done it more times. "Practice makes progress," she said. I found that interesting. We can't promise our kids they'll become perfect at something, even with lots and lots of practice. No one is perfect at everything, despite what you see on Pinterest boards. By using the word "progress," this mom helped her daughter realize that though she may not be great at something now, she can improve with repeated effort.

The less obvious message is that the popular trope of "you can be anything you want if you just try hard enough" is false. Despite this "good parenting" mantra of our modern culture, not everyone who wants to can become a Nobel Prize winner, or an astronaut, or Adele; which is why, when I sing at Mass, we suddenly end up with empty pews all around us. If your kids discover their big, fabulous dream isn't coming true, it's an opportunity to point out that God might not mean for them to cure the common cold, build a better mousetrap, invent a new ice cream flavor, save an endangered species, and all those things on the Game of Life "Life Tiles." Of course, you should encourage your kids to set reasonable goals, but remind them that if things don't seem to be working out, it may be because God has another, better plan that will take prayer and time to figure out. As an added bonus, fulfilling that plan will make them far happier even than winning *American Idol*. Pretending I did, however, comes in handy for those crowded Christmas and Easter Masses.

Seeing your children discouraged or disheartened is hard, though. Whenever a setback came to the children of a mom I know, she'd remind them that it just meant something great was about to happen. Many times I've witnessed sad endings being the path to happy beginnings. Like losing a job only to get a better one. Or, in kid language, their bike breaking and getting a new one. Maybe don't mention that to them, though, just in case their bike "accidentally" falls off a cliff. There are many highs and lows in life, but ultimately, God has our backs.

Leaving your children with an encouraging thought, such as God having it covered, is great at bedtime. Let them drift to sleep with something positive on their mind. My grandmother would always tell my mom, "You're wonderful" when tucking her in at night. "Jesus loves you, and I do too," you could say, especially if you butted heads that day, reminding your child that, despite everything, you still love him or her and always will.

You could also have them recall a happy thought from the day or remind them of something to look forward to the next day. (Perhaps not that last thing if they're the type to stay awake due to excitement.) Maybe they could fall asleep thinking about heaven, or what it would be like to ride on a giant eagle, or what the monster living under their bed looks like. Saint John Vianney's mom would speak to her children of God, Mary, and the angels before bed. Likewise, when they woke in the morning, she'd be there to remind them of Jesus, first thing.

Let the reminders continue. When a friend drops her kids off at school she tells them, "Be kind and always do your best." I respect that she goes beyond the cliché of "have fun" or "have a good day." You could even vary it up with things like "Be a friend to those who need it" or "Keep Jesus close in your thoughts" or "Remember that your guardian angel works for free so don't press your luck."

In the evening, try to make family dinner the norm. Being together strengthens the familial bond, builds positive relationships among siblings, and generally keeps teenagers out of the usual teenagery troubles. Younger kids learn new vocabulary words (for good or bad) and proper table manners. Everyone is more apt to eat healthy, and therefore be healthy, and you'll have a better idea what's going on in the lives of your kids. To get the ball rolling, you can play the high/low game where each person names the best and worst part of their day: "We bought a new carton of ice cream! That carton is now empty." It's a great way to find out what drives and motivates your kids.

Perhaps you're already familiar with Gary Chapman's book *The Five Love Languages*. He identifies them as: physical touch, words of encouragement, quality time, gift giving, and works of service. Chapman asserts that the way a person expresses love through one of those five methods is how he or she also feels love in return. Discovering someone's language makes it easier to show that person love. Mine must be acts of service, because I love my kids so much more when they do stuff for me.

This methodology also applies to children. Though, for my husband and me, it's difficult (especially when they're younger) to discern their love language unless it's physical touch. I have one like this. She'll often stop in front of me with her arms out and proclaim: "Hug Momma!" Then she'll latch on to me and make it hard to walk. Putting forth the effort to understand your kids' personalities is helpful for knowing what works and what doesn't with each child. Our oldest wrote us a nice note listing reasons why she loved us, which was very, very long, of course. Among her reasons was *not* hugging her when she's upset, or so she emphasized. Learning to accept the hands-off approach with her was difficult for us, but physical comfort only made things worse. (Later we found out writing this letter was her penance from confession, but we'll take it.)

This child's attitude, however, helped us learn another important lesson: not to make a mountain out of a molehill. When my kids hurt themselves, I'm kind of like, "meh." Yes, I'll tend to the wound, but I won't make a bigger deal out of it than it warrants. When I was a school secretary, kids would sometimes come to me asking for a Band-Aid for some microscopic cut. When I couldn't see anything, they'd squeeze until the tiniest drop of blood was visible. My favorite kids were the ones who came to the office with blood I could see from several feet away. I'd say, "Whoa, let me get you a Band-Aid," but they'd be like, "Nah, I'm just gonna slap a paper towel across it and head back out." Those kids were all from the same hardy family of goat owners. I loved them. The kids, not the goats. Maybe both. Baby goats are kids, so I guess both.

These children didn't try to make a huge fuss in order to get attention. They dealt with the problem simply and moved on. They were tough, and that's an attitude that will get them far in life. I recommend encouraging that in your kids, goat or human. For the whiners, ahem, I mean the more sensitive children, you can always point out that each passing moment gets the owie closer to being healed. You can also remind them that tomorrow they'll feel so much better (or by bedtime, or in like one minute, depending).

Something else helpful to keep in your back pocket is the phrase, "Would you like to be the one to" when asking a child to do something for you. That way it sounds like the requested task is an honor and a privilege rather than a chore, especially when you use this phrase with fun stuff. Would you like to be the one who puts the bubbles in the bathtub? Licks the sour cream spoon? Butters the garlic toast? Straightens the shoes? Puts away the laundry? Takes the trash to the dumpster? See what I did there? Sometimes that phrase kicks off something enticing. Whenever they hear it, their ears may perk. And if their answer is no, change the question to: "Put the laundry away or change the baby's stinky diaper? Those are your options." That laundry will get put away. Pretty much anything you couple with a stinky diaper will be guaranteed to get done.

Diaper changing duty is a task no kid would mind sharing with someone else without us needing to ask. Sharing, in general, however, shouldn't be forced. Even though "don't forget to share" is a common parental phrase, we shouldn't make our kids give up a toy or the swing for someone else all the time. Sharing is no doubt important, but only when the child does so from his own initiative. We can model sharing by doing so ourselves and then encouraging our kids to follow suit by pointing out how sharing brings others joy. For them you could say, "How nice of you to let the other boy play with your ball. See how happy you made him? Thank you for sharing."

However, sharing isn't always appropriate. What if your child wasn't finished on the swing, for instance? Instead, offer him advanced notice that soon it will be someone else's turn. "Five more minutes on the swing then let someone else have a go." Another option is playing together. "How about you kick the ball back and forth to each other?" rather than making your child give up his toy entirely. Being nice is one thing, but we don't want our children to feel like sharing is a punishment when they haven't done anything wrong.

Good parenting encompasses all these techniques. But just know that when all is calm and quiet in your home, and you're lulled into a false sense of security and "I'm a good parent"-ness, that's precisely when you'll find an entire roll of toilet paper unraveled into the toilet and a pile of poo sinking into the fibers of your bathroom rug. True story.

When you're feeling a little down, like you may be failing your children because they're not involved in fifty sports and you don't have thirty-two play dates lined up for next week, just ask yourself this: Are they happy (not just because you scored them tickets to WrestleMania on Ice) and holy (you're doing what you can there)? If yes, then you're a good parent. Be at peace.

CHAPTER THREE

Having Fun with Children ... Even Your Own!

"Waste time with your children so they
realize that love is always free."

• POPE FRANCIS •

As the mom, it's my duty to be the feeder, the cleaner, the make-sure-the-house-doesn't-burn-downer. Then Dad gets home from work, and all heck breaks loose as the kids drop whatever task they're completing for me to climb all over him.

But moms can be fun too. Right? I mean, that's what I've heard. Or is it just a rumor?

Normally I ascribe to the philosophy of never making eye contact with a happily playing child. Once spotted, you're forced to engage.

Then again, playing with your kids *can* actually be fun!

If you're into sports, as in, you actually enjoy them and so do your kids, you have it made. That shared interest can be a lot of fun for the whole family. A family, but not mine. The girls will occasionally attend my husband's basketball games. While he plays, they sit in the bleachers and read books. One of my daughters asked him, "Why don't you put us in sports?" He said, "Because you've shown absolutely zero interest in any sport, ever." She responded, "Yeah, that sounds right."

I didn't do sports as a kid. My older siblings played soccer, and I prayed wholeheartedly that I wouldn't have to also. God heard my prayer. That, or by the time it was my turn, being the youngest, my parents were too worn out to consider driving another kid to all those practices and games. Either way, it spelled relief for me.

A friend whose son enjoys soccer said to her, "Mommy, after soccer season ends, can you sign me up for flag football?" Being a good mom, she naturally responded in the affirmative. He continued: "And when I get to be in fifth or sixth grade, can you sign me up for tackle football?"

"Yes, we'll see."

"And then when I get grown up, can you sign me up for the NFL?"

Though I'm no athlete, it doesn't stop my friends, who wake up at 5:30 to run, from trying to convince me to join them. There must be something to it, though, as they seem very happy. Also insane, but crazy people do tend to laugh a lot, so it's hard to tell the difference.

My workout comes from lifting the baby on my legs while I lie on the floor. He cracks up and that makes me crack up too — until he drools into my mouth. But the beauty of that activity is the lying on the floor part. The girls and I do Wii Fit on occasion because it's more like playing than exercising. Except for the hula hoop game; that sucker gives my abs a workout. It wounds my stomach and my pride that my kids are so much better at it than I am.

At other times we exercise our ability to read a good book. I've read aloud to them many of the *Little House on the Prairie*, *Redwall*, *Lord of the Rings*, and *Chronicles of Narnia* series, as well as *Jennifer Lawrence's Guide to Submarine Building*. Sometimes we read outside. Being in nature is restorative mentally, and that's an added gift. Triple bonus if we're munching on healthy snacks. (Take that, soccer games! We can eat our orange slices at home!) Plus, while they listen, the girls smell flowers, look for bugs, or fashion sticks into weapons. This makes me a happy parent because we're all having fun and getting some vitamin D while we enjoy the great outdoors.

I like to insert my own words when reading to the kids to see if they're paying attention and whether or not I can fool them. It doesn't work, but I keep trying. I'll speak in my normal tone of voice to try to throw them off. "Nellie Oleson kept bothering Laura Ingalls, but then Aslan showed up and roared until Nellie ran away." They'll laugh and accuse: "Mom! It doesn't say that!"

This game sometimes backfires, however. When reading a book on choosing a cat for a pet to my then-six-year-old, I decided to embellish. "Cats are fun and playful just like Momma." This elicited a smile. "Cats are beautiful and smart just like Momma." Another smile. Phew. That was dangerous. Then my husband walked into the room and said, "Cats are furry and poop everywhere." To which my daughter added, with no hesitation: "Just like Momma!"

Reading to your children helps improve their vocabulary, which is fun as a parent to witness. For instance, my eight-year-old didn't say she was coming through the trees but that she was "emerging." Later she reported our chickens were "going haywire." My ten-year-old used the phrases "gain purchase" and "covering the same expanse." She also referred to the sunset as "the last dying embers of the great flame." Who *is* this kid? When I told my mom these things about her grandchildren so she could brag to her friends, as is my duty, she responded: "Must be nice having smart kids. We never had that." Thanks, Mom.

This reading helps foster that wondrous childhood creativity. As a parent to get in on that, you have to enter into the world of your children. Your first step is often getting down on the floor, which helps you feel like a kid again, and when is that ever not fun? Just be sure they help you back up before they run off to play something else.

Personally, I can only take so many tea parties and princess stories, but if coloring weren't fun for grown-ups, too, that adult coloring book craze would never have happened.

When your kids are old enough for board games, you're at a great stage. Chutes and Ladders drives me bananas, however, because just when you think it's finally going to be over, the person in the lead hits that big chute that takes you down to like, twelve. Somehow Candy Land is more tolerable. I remember my sister and me playing with my dad, which was unusual. The three of us were nearing King Kandy and the Candy Castle, and the game was almost over. However, the dreaded Plumpy card, which would send one of us back to the beginning, had yet to be drawn. We each picked our card haltingly, slowly turning it over, then heaving a sigh of relief when it was merely a color, perhaps a double color, but not the accursed Plumpy. The tension was finally broken by my dad crying, "This is so suspenseful!" My sister and I cracked up. I don't recall who won, but the memory is fond because it was odd for my dad to partake, much less get so into it. Do that for your kids — the unexpected.

As your children get older, more family games are possible, even if the youngest needs to pair up with a parent. We enjoy Tripoli, Apples to Apples Big Picture — with pictures instead of words — and Spoons. Growing up, Hearts was our go-to family card game. My siblings and I started a tradition of wearing baseball caps and then tipping them in acknowledgment when our score was read after each round. Now when we're home for a family reunion, the cards come out, and we scour our parents' house for hats so we can keep the tradition alive. It's absurd, but it's our thing. Every family should have that fun something that outsiders could never truly understand.

Any brand of silliness is bound to earn you points with your kids. My mom would often say, "You in the pink dress." No one was wearing a dress. Or pink. Once, I ate a blue Popsicle and showed the girls the spectacle of my blue tongue. They said, "Mooo-oomm!" in that same tone you use to admonish your kids for doing just such a thing, only they said it with a grin. Another time I put an M&M into each square (or triangle — it's of vital importance that you know each child's shape preference) of their peanut butter and jelly sandwich. Then I waited for their reaction: confusion, bewilderment, smiles, and once again: "Mooo-oomm!"

Another time the girls had a flotilla of paper boats on the living room floor. While they were out of the room, I put the boats on a blue blanket. When they returned, their boats were now on the ocean. I'd bunched up the blanket in lines like waves, with some boats riding them. Minds blown! And they could drag the blanket to their room to quickly and easily dock their boats where they belonged.

We have an interchangeable wall calendar like you find in elementary classrooms the world over. Our set came with holiday cards. When December rolled around, my husband daily switched the traditional, festive card meant for the twenty-fifth with a different holiday before he left for work. Each day the girls would be dismayed to find that their beloved holiday was changed to Memorial Day, Labor Day, even the Fourth of July. They'd come to me saying, "Mom, Christmas is the first day of summer vacation!" The next morning: "Now it's Groundhog Day!" The best was when my youngest said mournfully, "Christmas is now the worst day ever." You guessed it — the calendar showed "First day of school." I'm not sure who had more fun with this, the kids or my husband.

He also gets a kick out of surprising them every time we have a pasta meal by adding different shaped noodles to the pot. Suddenly their spaghetti turns into a treasure hunt for elbow macaroni, farfalle, mini shells, or alphabet pasta. We enjoy their exclamations of delight: "There's a bow tie in here! What is this, ziti? I found the letter G!"

Apparently hiding stuff is my husband's thing. It started with my birthday and a clue left at my spot at the table. That clue led to another, and another, each in its own hiding place until I found my birthday present. When he did this for one of the girl's birthdays too, I warned him, "You realize you're stuck now. Once you do it for one, you have to do it for them all, and for as long as they live here."

"Yeah, I know," he mourned.

But secretly he loves making and hiding these clues possibly even as much as the girls enjoy hunting them down. This activity also teaches the girls patience because he spreads out the clues and gifts throughout the day. One clue might say not to find the next one until after lunch, and then not until mid-afternoon, and so forth.

Similarly, because the kids don't need candy stuffed in all of those plastic eggs, one Easter we got creative. Some eggs had a piece of dry pasta, others contained mini chip clips, and if you think that's cruel, others contained pairs of their own underwear. If the girls didn't already know their parents were weird, well, the cat was out of the bag. They actually found this hilarious, proving they are our children.

My husband has also been known to bowl in the hallway with the girls by knocking down princess dolls instead of pins. (He must find it very satisfying.) If anyone topples Gustav from Frozen, he or she gets extra points since he's sturdier.

In addition to a plethora of princess dolls, my children have approximately 3.7 million stuffed animals. On my birthday I was presented with coupons to sleep with this or that animal for one, maybe even two weeks. The girls would even brush each animal's fur so that it looked its best for the important sleepover. Before I had baby Joe as my 6:00 a.m. alarm clock, I would occasionally — okay, daily — wake up after my girls. When I'd hear them coming to get me, I'd grab whatever chosen animal I had been loaned at the time and snuggle it under my arm like it had been there all night. Their squeals of delight earned me major bonus points.

I will hug and kiss all their animals as often as they like, except for The Crow. I've chosen to have an unholy dislike for this particular foul beast. Knowing this, the girls just love making him pop up unexpectedly on my pillow, in a kitchen cabinet, or in my underwear drawer. They've even had him land on me from behind, giggling at my alarm and feigned panic of being attacked by my foe. Consequently, this "game" has been going on for years.

Another of our silly games involves Japanese artist Katsushika Hokusai (1760–1849) whom we learned about in my daughter's art class. For reasons unknown, we took an intense liking to the name Hokusai. For reasons further unknown, I suggested to the girls that when their dad got home, they should jump out and say "Hokusai!" Of course they eagerly agreed, and when my husband arrived, he was bewildered and wondered what oddity their mother had come up with now. To this day, the younger two girls do their best to sneak up on and "Hokusai" me. Sometimes they'll say "Hokusai?" as in, "Did I succeed in surprising you?" It may be one of the most bizarre games ever invented, but they'll perhaps cherish it forever. My grandchildren may one day play it, but hopefully not to the point of giving their grandpa a heart attack.

If silly fun doesn't liven things up around your home, try music. Baby Joe has dinosaur pajamas with dino feet, complete with toes/claws that stick out. That, coupled with my daughter building a city out of foam blocks, meant I just had to help Joe destroy that city, with my daughter's permission, as the lyrics "Oh! No! There goes Tokyo! Go, go, Godzilla!" from the band Blue Oyster Cult played. He had no idea what was happening, but the rest of us were cracking up.

Music plays a large role in peoples' emotions, and I'm not just talking rom-coms with sad music when the couple has a falling out and it's raining — it's always raining. I read somewhere that when David danced before the Ark of the Covenant, Saul's hardened heart was softened. The music in praise of the Lord drove out the spirit of anger in Saul. Perhaps a little Christian praise and worship will drive out the spirit of crazy in your kids and bring peace to your home.

If it's literally, or figuratively, raining outside, make it a grand time inside by putting on some upbeat tunes. I dance like no one's watching, because, apparently, my kids don't count. When they see me grooving, I like to think it's an unexpected treat. Their laughter is that of sheer joy. I mean, that can be the only reason they laugh when they see me dance, right? I love grabbing their hands and having them join in. I taught my eight-year-old to swing dance to a Bob Dylan song because, why not?

Some of my fondest memories growing up are when the couch and chairs would be pushed back and my dad would put on some records. We kids would join in or just sit back and enjoy Mom and Dad cutting a rug. At a church dance, the crowd actually formed a circle around my parents to watch them break it down. I was so proud. Even if you're no Beyoncé, dancing is a fun family activity that will hopefully become happy memories for your kids who don't care if you dance well or not. And when they get older, because you're their parents, they won't expect you to be good dancers. When they're teenagers, if you want them to leave the room, just turn on some music and show 'em your moves.

If you're rearranging furniture anyway, why not make a fort with couch cushions and blankets? Have you ever ducked inside of it when the kids weren't around, only to have them delight in finding you? Maybe they won't notice that you've fallen asleep. For future reference, forts are also handy when a child needs his own space to decompress, or get homework done in a fun place all his own with fewer distractions.

If you want to get out of the house, libraries are great at providing activities for kids. I enjoyed craft Wednesdays during the summer with mine. You can always google fun things to do in your area for more ideas, like nature hikes or little-known museums, perhaps restaurants that serve unusual cuisine since kids are great at trying new foods, as everyone knows.

When you're out with your kids but not your spouse, try having him or her join you by secret prearrangement. My husband did this at the grocery store. As he came sauntering down the aisle toward us, the girls flipped out like they hadn't seen him in years. I caught onlookers smiling. If any of them had judged us for our family size, they couldn't deny our love for one another. Who wouldn't want lots of children when it means that much more love to go around?

Pets are great for family bonding and teaching children responsibilities. We raise chickens, which means the kids need to refill the water and food bins, scoop the coop poop, and best yet, look for eggs. They bond with the birds, and, I suspect, secretly have their favorites. It makes me happy that our food scraps can be repurposed as chicken feed rather than thrown away. I suppose a dog would work for that purpose just as well, except for the leftover chocolate. Like anyone ever has leftover chocolate.

Perhaps equally enriching and fulfilling is planting a family garden. Having read *Little House on the Prairie* to my girls may have motivated them to help "Pa" till the soil, plant the seeds, and water the crops. Wandering outside for a snack or to collect salad items is such a buzz for me. I also love being able to say to the girls, "You're hungry? Then go outside." At certain times of year there are plenty of fruits and veggies for them to dine on. Additionally, my youngest daughter has become an expert at homemade lemonade from our trees — a perk for the whole family.

A study conducted for Britain's Royal Horticultural Society lists more benefits to gardening. The research found that teaching children gardening improves their development by making them happier, more self-assured, more patient, and better able to handle adversity. Raising home-grown food also teaches them healthy eating. If you have the yard for it, or space on a patio for planter boxes, I highly encourage gardening with your kids.

Though I'm hesitant to recommend shows, Studio C on YouTube has been enjoyable for our family. It's sketch comedy that's actually clean. Did you know such a thing existed? Start with season 1 because the earlier seasons are the best. Of course you should preview them before showing your children. Quoting our favorite episodes (each one is about three-to-five minutes) has brought us laughter and inside jokes. In addition to entertainment, it's created a family bond.

Undoubtedly you already do enjoyable activities with your

children. These are just a few of the things we do with ours. Every now and then, ignore the dishes, the chores, and the strict bedtime. Drop everything and go on a walk, or go fishing, or make a backyard bonfire and roast s'mores. If it's the wrong time of year, use your indoor fireplace or even a gas stove and eat s'mores in February. This kind of spontaneity is what having fun with kids is all about.

Think back on your childhood. What do you remember fondly? Is it the silly little games? The quirky traditions that were unique to your family? The enjoyment you have together, even in the small things, will form the overall impression of a happy childhood. Doing that for your kids makes you a fun, and happy, parent.

CHAPTER FOUR

Tears and Temper Tantrums – What to Do When Your Kids Are Crying Too

"In certain difficult moments, a humble prayer to God is much more useful than a violent outburst of anger."

• SAINT JOHN BOSCO •

How best to handle tears and whining can be summed up in one word: Oreos. I'm talking a Costco-sized box hidden in the depths of your closet where you can close the door behind you and dig in.

I actually heard of a woman who does this. I might be jealous. But there may be less caloric options for coping with crying kids.

For starters, here's a useful knowledge-nugget from psychologist and family physician Dr. Leonard Sax. In his book, *Why Gender Matters: What Parents and Teachers Need to Know About the Emerging Science of Sex Differences,* he states that children are physically unable to use words to explain why they're sad. The area of the brain that holds negative emotions, the amygdala, doesn't move those emotions into the prefrontal cortex, which handles higher learning and thought processes, until adolescence in girls, and never in boys. Teenage girls can easily tell you why they're upset; boys cannot. For parents this means asking our children what's wrong or why they're upset can be a frustrating experience for both us and them. Knowing this, we can save ourselves some trouble by coming up with methods to work out the cause of our children's crankiness.

I discovered that my husband and I tend to get cranky because of one of two things: for me, fatigue; for my husband, hunger. Figuring this probably applies to children also, when one is uncharacteristically cranky, I ask, "Are you tired? Did you not get enough sleep? Want to lie down and rest for a bit?" Then silently to myself, "Oh, please, oh, please, oh, please." Or, "Are you hungry? Need a snack?" With younger kids, it's harder to determine their weaknesses. Crankiness happens. But once you develop a sense of what triggers crankiness in your children, you might be able to head off the insanity by having a granola bar at the ready to toss at them as to a trained seal.

If your child is the tired and cranky type, particularly at the purgative stage of not needing another nap but not quite able to make it to bedtime, you may need to adopt a "Why don't we snuggle on the couch with a blanket and a book" plan. This is also the way to go at certain times when a child complains of being bored. You think, he has books, games, siblings, and instructions for building his own submarine. How could he be bored? The problem may be that he's too awake to sleep, but too sleepy to do anything. He may actually be saying, "I'm feeling out of sorts, and I don't know why. Help!" Quiet time with Mom or Dad is an effective remedy. Maybe reading a book to him will be enough to send him re-energized out into the day. And for your teenager who complains of being bored, hand him a rag and bucket and tell him to wash the car.

Give your kids latitude when they're tired or cranky. When

my husband and I were dating, we had dinner with a family who had young children. One little boy was having a difficult time making it through the meal without moaning, sighing, and fidgeting. His dad chastised him and ultimately sent him to his room. The mom tried to calm the dad's irritation by explaining that the little boy hadn't slept well and was just tired. She wanted her husband to take it easy on their son, but to no avail.

As a guest witnessing this, it was a little awkward. It also reminded me of the time I was in a very "off" mood as a kid. I was acting weird and I knew it, but I couldn't seem to help myself. Not understanding or sympathizing, my dad also yelled at me, which made me act all the weirder. Ultimately, I too was sent to my room. I relate this to how you're not supposed to honk when someone makes a mistake while driving. Chances are good that the person knows he did something wrong. Honking will only make him flustered, possibly resulting in yet another driving error. Knowing this, if your kids are tired and crabby, yelling or scolding them will likely make matters worse. Try the other evasive maneuvers listed in this chapter before enacting discipline. Being patient and paying attention will help you treat the situation properly for a child who just needs a nap, some quiet time, or to be held for a few minutes.

That snuggly time with a parent works wonders when little kids are tired or crying over everything from owies, to a broken toy, to trying to fit the rudder on their submarine. The best method I've found for quieting those tears is a rocking chair or glider in a darkened room. I'll swoop that kid up in my arms, grab her blanket and teddy bear, and hold her in my lap, rocking silently for several minutes. When the crankiness subsides, I wait a few minutes longer, and then ask in a hushed tone, "Do you feel better? Would you like to go back out now?" If she says yes, we rejoin society, refreshed and renewed. If she needs a little more cozy quiet time with Mom, so be it. Either way, when we leave the room, she's happy again, and therefore I am also.

Singing helps quiet my cranky little boy. When he's not keen on having his diaper changed, I sing, "It's diaper changing time," to the tune of "The Farmer in the Dell." I used to sing to my girls before naps as part of their sleep routine. When the first daughter was getting a little older, I asked, "Do you still want me to sing to you?" She replied, "No," a little too quickly. I stopped singing to any of the girls after that. They may have been trying to tell me something, though at least not as overtly as a friend whose daughter said to him, "When you sing, God cries."

Humor is another tool that can help steady a quivering lip. When my siblings and I would stub our toes on the couch, trip over the rug, or run into the wall (apparently we were a clumsy lot), my mom would admonish the offending inanimate object. "Shame on you, wall! How dare you hurt my Betsy's toe! Bad wall!" I do it with my kids now, too. Is clumsiness hereditary? It doesn't make them "LOL," but it sometimes earns me a snicker and the tears let up. Maybe they're just confused (is Mom clumsy *and* losing her mind?) but it nevertheless distracts them from crying. Sometimes my husband and I will tell our girls to run cold water on an owie or put it against a soft fuzzy blanket or stuffed animal. We don't know whether or not it works for them, but they run off to do it, so it works for us.

If it isn't tears, it's complaining. I tell my children they're not allowed to complain if they're not willing to do anything to change their situation. Like if they grumble about being cold, but refuse to get up and put on a sweater. Or they want to go trick-or-treating with their fellow preschoolers but won't sew themselves a costume. I won't tolerate that sort of laziness in my home. When the solution to their problem is simple, but they won't enact the change, complaining is verboten. If, on the other hand, they sigh longingly because there's only one of me to love, they get a cookie.

The sister of complaining is whining: my biggest pet peeve. Sometimes I tell my kids I can't understand them when they're whining, which is true and also motivates them to speak coherently if they hope to get anything out of me. I also tell them I can only handle one cranky child at a time. Also true. So when the baby is crying and they want to whine or complain, I tell them to wait their turn.

My other rule is, if you want to whine, do it in your room. Knowing this, my seven-year-old, complaining her way through her math worksheets, finally stopped and said, "I'll go in the other room so you don't have to hear me." Yelling at them to stop whining is about as useful as telling someone of any age to "Calm down!" or as effective as getting your kids to shut the van door if they're the last one out. Instead, in as gentle a tone as I can muster, I'll say something like, "Sweetheart, you're whining," then look at her pointedly, waiting for her to either speak normally or get out of hearing range.

If she opts for the latter and stomps off crying to her room, I let her. Before when I'd send a kid to her room to whine in private, or for being bad, I'd sometimes punish her further if she slammed her door. I've since learned this doesn't help either of us. In fact, it just makes us both more upset. So, I let her slam the door if it makes her feel better, and stomp all she wants along the way. It's irritating, sure, but doesn't do any real harm. Once there, she can throw her stuffed animals across the room. Then feel guilty, pick them up, and hug them to apologize (I'm sure). But squeezing a beloved stuffed animal helps make kids feel better. Good preschool and kindergarten teachers know this and keep cute cuddlies at the ready.

Back to my child. When the crying has died down, I sit on the other side of the door, gently scratch my nails against it, and quietly "meow." If your child is more into puppies, I'm sure a gentle "woof woof" would work as well. If elephants are your kid's thing, trumpet your heart out. If he's into giraffes, well, you're on your own there.

Once I have my daughter's attention, I wiggle my fingers under the door and suddenly pull them back out. I repeat this in different places — one end of the door, then the other, the middle, etc. This turns into a game where she tries to catch my fingers. Once I feel hers on mine, I gasp and quickly pull my fingers away. You know you've done the job well when you hear giggles. When she gets tired of catching my hand, she sticks hers through, and the game goes in reverse. After a while, it's time to open the door for snuggles right there on the floor until all is well again.

Sometimes you can avoid sending a child to his room, and the ensuing walk of a thousand deaths down the hallway, with some consoling words and straight-up sympathy. Consider this scenario: Baby Joe knocked down Youngest Daughter's block tower. She started crying and complaining that it would take *forever* to rebuild. I responded, "It will take two minutes tops! Besides, wasn't building it the fun part?" Amazingly, my stellar logic didn't stop the tears even a little. What could I, clearly a perfect mother, have done differently? Observe:

"Mom, Jojo broke my tower!"

Me, kneeling down to her level: "I'm sorry, honey. That probably took a long time to build, didn't it? (Knowing it didn't is immaterial. It may have felt long to her.) I wrap my arms around her.

Her: Tears and nodding.

"I'm sorry your baby brother knocked it down."

Sniffle.

"I'm sure he didn't mean to."

Sniffle, nod.

"If I move him farther away, would you like to rebuild it?"

Nod, sniffle. Releases me from hug, wipes tears away.

Perhaps a little more consoling would've been required to reach this outcome, but you get the idea. Kids want to have their feelings validated rather than simply dismissed. Acknowledge that you get they're bummed, you understand, you sympathize. Something akin to "Suck it up and deal" is not a winner. However, "Dude, that stinks. I feel for you," is pretty much up there with, "I love you," or "I brought dessert," when it comes to powerful phrases for kids. Actually, they mean the same thing to them. Okay, and to me. Walking away and letting them cry it out is one way to go if you don't mind hearing the tears; but stopping what you're doing to show you care is being a good parent with a happier kid. We're talking young kids here. As they get older, you can determine when they ought to be able to work things out on their own. "Mom, stop hugging me. The pizza delivery taking forty-five minutes is not that big of a deal."

When our girls were younger, my husband and I took them to the annual pumpkin patch, which was followed by the annual "Why do we keep doing this?" conversation on the way home. The pumpkin patch meant mini rides, inflatable houses, a petting zoo, and empty wallets by the time we reached the car. The wrapping-up portion of the program also meant meltdowns. We'd respond with the ever-helpful, "Why are you crying? You had a great time. Don't be ungrateful or we won't do fun things like this again." Obviously, that threat worked well, since we continued to go back year after year. Then I realized something important: it wasn't ingratitude they were expressing, it was disappointment that the fun was over. Sometimes we're a little thick.

And so the sympathy play begins again:

"I'm sorry we have to leave. You were having fun, weren't you?"

Sobs all around. "Ye-e-esssss!"

"It's hard when you have to stop playing."

Nod, sob.

"You wish we could stay longer?"

Sniffle, nod.

"I'm sorry, but the nice people who work there need to go home to eat dinner and so do we."

Now they may be feeling for the workers, understanding all too well the desire to eat when hungry. Encouraging empathy is also a winner. The point is, acknowledging their emotions makes them feel they have worth. Showing you understand goes a long way to drying those tears.

Another option is saying, "Wouldn't it be nice if when we're having fun, time stood still? If only I had a magic wand, I would make it so no time passed when we're playing and you could just keep on having a great time forever. I wish I was a fairy godmother." Pantomime waving a wand in the air if you're up for it. "Bippity. Boppity. Boo. Darn. It didn't work. Do you want to try?

Do you have a magic wand I don't know about? Where are you hiding it?" You can check her back, up her sleeve, her tummy, etc. That ought to get her laughing, or at least smiling enough to ease the tears.

Perhaps you've heard of the tactic where your child is freaking out and you place a box of crayons and a stack of paper in front of him saying, "Show me how you feel." This works especially well for younger children who can't vocalize well. Let him grab a black crayon and scribble angrily all over that first sheet of paper. And the second. And the third, and so on, until he's scribbled himself out and feels better. A word of caution though: use this technique sparingly. The effect can wear off if your child is on to this "trick" and no longer wishes to participate.

Worse than whining and crying are temper tantrums. When they happen at home, you can do your best to defuse the situation with one of the previously mentioned methods, or you can chuck the kid in his room and walk away. When my friend's son throws a fit in the car for not getting his way, she cranks up the radio to drown him out. It's no fun to scream for attention and be ignored, so what's the point in continuing? If your child just needs to get it out of his system, so be it, but you don't have to be tortured by it. If it's my own child torturing me, I'll return the favor by singing along to whatever's playing. When you act oblivious to screaming children, it deflates their misbehaving balloon and teaches them that temper tantrums get them nowhere.

Tantrums outside the house or car, like in the grocery store, are another animal entirely. One little girl, when her mom wouldn't let her have a sample at Costco, screamed nonstop. Another woman, undoubtedly a mother too, approached this poor, distressed mom and said, "What can I do?" The mom tore her shopping list in half and said, "You get this half. I'll get the other and meet you in the front." And the woman did it, enabling the mom to get her shrieking kid out of the store that much sooner. Way to go, lady. Help a sista out.

Since kids take advantage of their parents' fear of public discipline, my advice, is to not worry about onlookers. When you're focused on your child, you may see adult legs nearby, but don't raise your gaze. Those bodies around you (potentially busybodies at that) should remain fuzzy, unfocused shapes in your periphery. Remember that many of those adults are parents who've been in your position and they'll understand. Maybe one will shoot you a sympathetic look, but I wouldn't risk eye contact. If someone glances at you reprovingly, it will only upset you more. And those childless adults who want to judge you have no frame of reference, and therefore no right to pass judgment on your parenting. Pretend they're not there.

If your child has been taken in by the throes of an evil tantrum, you can begin with some low-grade defense mechanisms like the earlier suggestion of establishing the root cause of this attack: "Whoa, kid. What's the matter? Are you tired? Do you want to ride in the cart instead of walking?" If that's not working, try, "Want a snack?" Hopefully you brought something with you. If not, tear open a bag off the nearest shelf. (And buy the bag, of course.) If it happens to be dog treats, well, that will teach him a lesson. (Kidding!) Then while he's halfway through that Super Yum-Yum Happy Bar, you can casually lift him and put him in the cart "for safe keeping."

The next level of self-destruct mode happens when he doesn't want to get in the cart and smacks your proffered gift away because it's not the true object of his desire: a beautiful jar of Marshmallow Milk Chocolate Peanut Butter Skittles and Milk Dud Fluff. (I almost threw up just typing that.) Play the sympathy card again. "That does look good doesn't it?" (Hurk!) "There are a lot of yummy things in this store. Too bad we don't have the money to buy all the delicious fun things, but maybe we can get one on a special day. Can you think of any special days we can celebrate with something extra special like that Marshmallow Fluff?"

Thinking … thinking … "My birthday?"

"Sure! What a great idea! Let's get this for you on your birthday!" Secretly hoping he'll forget by then.

"Can't we get it today?"

"But today is just a *normal* day. Something as wonderful and terrific as that (hard swallow) Fluff deserves to be enjoyed on a super special day like your birthday. Let's try to hurry up and finish our shopping so we can go home and look at the calendar. Then we can count down the days until your birthday."

"Can't we look on your phone?"

"Okay, but you have to be in the cart to look at my phone."

"Why?"

"Because if you walk while looking at my phone, you might run into something or someone. Let's be on the safe side," you say while picking him up before any further discussion can happen.

If those sweet-talking negotiations break down, move on to the next phase: Operation Cobra. Or tougher still: Operation Platypus. For me, this meant holding my daughter firmly by the wrist to make her face me. To casual onlookers we were having a staring contest. Little did they know my look said, "You will stop misbehaving this instant and come with me right now." I might then ask, "Are you going to be good?" If I got a nod, we'd be on our merry way. If not, I continued holding and staring until she gave the correct answer. This way, she knew I was in charge and her behavior was neither appreciated nor tolerated.

If the situation reaches DEFCON Three: chase after and grab your kicking, screaming child, toss him in the cart and get the heck out of there. Being firm and not backing down may be a hassle, but remaining in charge goes a long way toward preventing future attacks. If an ornery child can't get away with anything, why would he bother continuing to try? Don't be a push-over parent like the ones in the checkout lines who say no over and over to a child begging and pleading for those devilishly ill-placed candy bars at children's eye level. One "no" is sufficient. All other supplications are to be ignored. If necessary, add, "I said no, now put it back." Onlookers will be impressed by your backbone. My mom reports witnessing a parent saying "no" after each "pretty please" and finally, "Okay, but that's the last time I'm buying this for you." Until next time. If you establish that no always means no, there won't be a next time.

Whatever you do, take the advice of Saint John Bosco at the start of this chapter and say a little prayer for help with each encounter. And then a deep breath. But while you're out, don't forget to replenish your secret Oreo supply.

CHAPTER FIVE

The Dreaded D-Word – Discipline

"Long experience has taught me that patience is the only remedy for even the worst cases of disobedience."

• SAINT JOHN BOSCO •

My parents were leisurely wandering through their small town's street fair one afternoon, stopping by booths that caught their eye, and occasionally picking up promotional items, a.k.a. swag, when my mom felt a tug on the bag she was holding, one she'd been given somewhere along the way. She looked down to see a young girl trying to pull the bag out of her hand. She was too bewildered to respond. Then the girl's parents rushed up to her.

"Where did you find that bag?" The mom asked, frantic. "We need to find one right away."

Mystified, my mom pointed. "At a booth back that way."

"Okay. We'll get you one, sweetie. It's okay. We're getting one for you right now," and they hurried off.

My parents, shaking their heads, watched them go.

"I feel so bad for that girl's parents," Mom told me.

"Forget the parents," I said. "They dug their own grave. I feel sorry for that child. One day she's going to grow up and realize the world doesn't revolve around her and she can't have everything she wants. It will be a rude awakening. Her parents are doing her a major disservice."

My mom, since of course she did a stupendous job raising me, had to agree. Spoiling a child does no one any good. It just makes life miserable for the parents who become afraid of their child, and the kid becomes a haughty, selfish brat with no self-control. Clearly, this little girl's parents lacked discipline — for her, and for themselves.

In the book *The Story of the Trapp Family Singers*, Maria Von Trapp of *The Sound of Music* fame, shared that when she transitioned from governess to mom, she laid down some ground rules. There were three items her children were not permitted to play with, she told them: scissors, matches, and, actually I forget the third thing, so let's say explosives.

"No scissors, matches, or dynamite," she told them.

Then one of the girls, Agathe, walked by the next day with scissors. Maria had to stop her, take the scissors away, and remind her, "No scissors."

The next day Agathe did it again, this time with matches. Maria again had to stop her and reprimand her with the appropriate punishment.

The third day Agathe had the nerve to walk past Maria carrying a brick of C4 with a remote cell phone detonator. Maria stopped her, punished her, and said, "I told you no scissors, matches, or incendiary devices. Why did you blatantly disobey me?"

Agathe responded, "I needed to be sure you meant it."

Isn't that the truth? Kids will test us. If you lay out the repercussions for misbehavior, you'd better be willing and able to follow through. If your child knows your chosen consequence is unrealistic, your discipline will be ineffective. You must be consistent, practical, and timely about carrying out the prescribed punishment. Also, a good rule of thumb is the number of minutes a child spends in time-out (or suffering any other conse-quence) should be equal to his age. If your college student comes home for a visit, putting him in time-out will give you *loads* of quiet time.

If the rules are clear-cut, no room is left for negotiation and haggling — potentially weakening your resolve, leading a child on a path of getting away with anything. Have rules in place and stick with them: this much screen time, this much gaming time, this many snacks or sweets allowed in a day, this is the curfew, this is how long you can spend praising the greatness of your parents (as a minimum, not a maximum). When the rule is there with no waffling, children stop crying, whining, and pleading, because they understand that doing so will get them nowhere. You, as the parent, won't waste time considering your response to these questions, nor be swayed by their doe eyes. Ultimately, they'll learn they can't walk all over you.

Unfortunately, society has made parenting more difficult. Nowadays, parents are expected not to tell children what they'll be doing, but to ask them what they want to do, almost like they're co-parents. Fortunately, you're the parent, and you get to make the rules. For instance, in our home, if there's an extra serving of dessert, I get to eat it. I benevolently do this on Joe's behalf. He's too young, so he'll get it in my milk. What more excuse do I need for breast-feeding?

One way to make sure your kids know you're in charge is to not end commands with "okay?" This makes it sound like you're asking a question or that responding in the negative is an option. Don't say, "It's time to go, okay?" Your child might think (and express), "Not okay." So instead, make a statement. "We're leav-ing the park in five minutes so start gathering your things now." Then have your child say, "Yes, Mommy," or, "Yes, Daddy." This way he can't claim he didn't hear you. Pretty slick, no? It also reinforces obedience and respect.

When I've asked the kids to do something like get dressed or clean their room, and instead find them playing — still in their pj's and a messy room — I say, "Do you think I'm a happy Momma or a sad Momma right now?" Since they aren't monsters and have learned the value of keeping Mom happy, they generally get dressed right away. Better yet, I've learned to let them know I'm coming down the hallway by announcing it and walking slowly so they can quickly get dressed. Then they've done what was asked, no discipline needed.

Also, rather than repeat over and over, "Go get dressed," try, "What are you supposed to be doing right now?" If they give the wrong answer, suggest they try again. Better yet, don't tell them to do something, just point out what needs to be done with neutral instead of negative statements. Rather than, "You didn't shut the door," say, "The door is still open." A simple reminder, without the negativity, will get the job done. Even better, when possible, just say their name and point to what needs to be done. They can't accuse you of nagging them, you hardly said a word! And in doing so, they don't feel belittled. You could even be cute about it by clearing your throat and tilting your head toward shoes left in the middle of the floor, maybe giving one a little shove in your child's direction. The fewer words you have to say, the better. Your kids won't feel belittled, you won't feel like you're constantly telling them what to do, and your relationship with your child will benefit.

When your child doesn't want to do the task you've asked him to do, perhaps you can benevolently suggest he do two different tasks instead. If he chooses those, now you've gotten two chores accomplished for the price of one. And, of course, there's always the classic "dirty diaper" approach mentioned earlier, where you provide options: one being the thing you want to get done, the other being something much worse. "You can either vacuum this room or give the cat a bath — cat style." This works with food as well. "You can either eat this or an octopus sandwich." Admittedly, that could backfire. Or, "You have to at least try it. You can have an elephant-sized bite or a mouse-sized bite. You choose."

Alternatively, when your child wants to do something you would prefer him or her not to do, instead of forbidding it, explain the consequences such as, "Okay, you can play video games instead of doing your homework, but that means you're going to spend Saturday helping Grandpa clip his chickens' toenails."

Whatever your instructions may be, make sure they're clear. At 10:00 on Sunday mornings, the girls need to get ready for church. My husband said to them one weekend, "Girls, it's ten."

No movement.

"You need to tell them what that means," I said.

My husband clarified. "Girls, it's ten o'clock, which means the short hand is on the ten and the long hand is on the twelve."

My eighth-grade English teacher told us that when dinner was ready and he or his wife called their kids to the table, if the kids chose to keep playing rather than come, the parents ate without them. And once dinner was over, the kitchen was closed. It only took the mistake of not coming when they were called once for the children to learn. At the time, I thought that was harsh. Now, as a parent, I think it's brilliant.

Getting your kids to do what you want is one thing, but what about persuading them not do something, like hitting? One method that works well is to say, "We don't do that in this family" or "Kerekeses don't do that." Input your own last name, however, lest your child ask you what a Kerekes is, and that's a conversation no one wants to have. But pointing out that your child is a part of the family, and that the family has a certain set of values, makes him feel special. Reminding your kids how members of the family behave makes their little minds want to fit in, especially when it implies being like looked-up-to older siblings.

Another trick is to ask your children if their saintly namesake would behave this way, as in, "Would Saint Matthew do this?" Or … maybe not. Bad example. "Would Saint Paul—" Darn. That could work against you, too. Hopefully you've named your children after saints without a colorful past. If you haven't had any children yet, I recommend just going with the names John and Theresa for all of them. I have noticed that when I pull this stunt (I mean, try this) with my misbehaving children, they feel a kinship with their saint and actually pause to consider not wanting to disappoint said saint.

If you're the mom and your children aren't listening to you, lower your voice an octave. Boys, especially, respond better to lower voices. My husband doesn't always understand the power of his dad voice. When our girls were doing something he didn't approve of, he'd say, "Stop. Stop. Stop." I told him he didn't have to say it three times. Once would get the job done. He responded, "Okay, okay, okay."

When it comes to bad behavior, psychologists say the goal is for your children to feel guilt rather than shame. Guilt means they did something bad. Shame means they feel like a bad person, which is much tougher to correct. We don't want them to feel small. That's a lasting emotion they may begin to believe defines them. If you react to a child's mistake with anger, they'll feel shame. Disappointment, on the other hand, brings about a feeling of guilt. Along with expressing your disappointment, you can let your child know not only what he or she did wrong, but how it affected others, promoting empathy as well as responsibility. And finally, you can teach or demonstrate how to correct the wrong. Ultimately, this gives the impression that the child is still a good person who made a mistake, but who can do better next time.

The bottom line is to be patient with kids. Take note of the quote from Saint John Bosco at the start of this chapter: "Long experience has taught me that patience is the only remedy for even the worst cases of disobedience." He elsewhere pointed out that it's so much easier to lose one's patience than to control one's patience. I'm sure every parent has experienced that.

Léonie Martin, an older sister of Saint Thérèse of Lisieux, was a problem child. Saint Zélie, her mom, was relieved to send her to boarding school, where Léonie's aunt, a nun, could look after and try to fix her. Her aunt scolded her for every wrong-doing, to the point where the rebukes were basically constant with no changes in behavior. She then decided to change tactics and became kind and loving to Léonie, instead. The difference was remarkable. With patience and gentleness, Léonie strove to make her aunt proud, eventually becoming a nun herself — and is now a Servant of God, possibly to be canonized one day!

One of my girls was an especially stubborn and difficult toddler. When she preferred her applesauce on the kitchen cabinets, counter, and nearby carpet fibers than in her stomach, I wanted to yank my hair out. Gradually she improved and is now my sweetest, most loving and obedient girl. If you have difficult children, take heart. One day you may discover that he's no longer a problem for you, even if only because it's his wedding day and he's now his wife's problem. At least you managed to get him in marriageable shape.

Remember that though you have to be firm in your discipline, you should be equally affectionate so your kids know you love them no matter what. After an altercation with your child, hug him or her for at least six seconds. This is the minimum amount of time needed for a chemical in the body to be released, letting one know that everything is okay again. (Pro-tip: this works with your spouse too!)

Finding this balance between discipline and affection is a key to happiness because it forms kids who will be easier to manage and won't drive you nuts ... well, not quite as nuts. My guiding principle since my first child has been to expect good behavior and accept nothing less. When they don't comply, gently show them the proper way to behave. In time, they'll get there. And you'll both be happier for it.

CHAPTER SIX

Cleaning Up

"To convert somebody [into a good cleaner] go
and take them by the hand and guide them."

• SAINT THOMAS AQUINAS •

with a nearly flawless, undetectable addition by the author

In my high school art class, I sat next to a guy who would routinely toss his used paint brushes into the sink, rather than clean them as we were instructed to do. One time I finally asked him, "Why aren't you washing your brushes?" He said, "Someone else will get it." I had no response to that, at least not one that would be polite. I knew this kid was from a wealthy family, probably with a maid, so he was accustomed to "someone else getting it." I can only imagine what his dorm room must've been like in college. And not caring, or perhaps knowing how, to clean up after himself was undoubtedly a winning trait for his future wife. (Yes, that was sarcasm.)

In more recent history, my family went to a friend's house for dinner. When I say house, mansion would be a more accurate description. As their two young children played, the housekeeper moved along behind them, picking up and putting away discarded dolls and dress-up clothes before they had time to grow cold. Those two little girls never had to give their toys a second glance. On the way home, I remarked to my husband that those girls probably didn't know a thing about cleaning. Unless they marry rich, they'll be in trouble when it comes to tending their own home without a maid.

My husband is a teacher, and occasionally he'll hear a kid brag to his friends that he doesn't have to do chores, to which my husband will say to him, in front of his peers, "I feel sorry for you."

We do our children a disfavor when we don't give them chores. Doing tasks around the house teaches kids valuable skills for taking care of themselves and keeping their future homes from being condemned by the sanitation police. Chores also improve kids' self-esteem, giving them a healthy form of pride for completing a task successfully. Helping around the house provides a sense of being part of, and an important contributor to, the family. Studies show that kids who do chores have a greater concern for others. Plus, chores teach them time management when homework or sports are thrown into the mix.

Learning the balance between work and play, as in, you get your work done and then you play, is an invaluable skill that will serve your kids well in life. Unfortunately, few to zero children actually enjoy doing work.

My oldest often laments having to do schoolwork or wash dishes or sniff the cheese to see if it's gone bad; she just wants to write her novel. I tell her I get that — big time — but we don't get to do what we want until we finish our work first. So open up that cheese bag, brace yourself, and take a big whiff. Life, in general, is about doing the work first so we can "play" afterward in heaven. If you spend your time on earth doing nothing but playing, you don't get the reward of heaven. I let her chew on that for a while. And the cheese, in case the sniff test was inconclusive.

A solid work ethic developed through doing chores will help your children appreciate their tidy home, too, though they're probably unlikely to admit it. They'll secretly enjoy the clean house, for so long as it lasts, all the more knowing they helped make it happen. But most of all, less clutter equals less chaos, which equals happier parents. Living in an orderly home is always sweeter when you know your kids did the cleaning instead of you. Sure, you may have to inspect or spruce up a bit, but the bulk of the work wasn't done by you!

Eventually no more sprucing will be needed, but getting your family to that point takes patience. Often it's easier to do the task yourself rather than training your children to do it competently, but we shouldn't do for the child what the child can, with a little guidance, do for himself. If you complete even simple tasks for him, he won't learn, or discover what he's capable of. Give him the opportunity to gain knowledge, rather than rely on others. For me, this means daily yelling across the house: "Whoever went last needs to come flush the toilet!"

Every child is different, of course, but here are some suggestions for age-appropriate chores to use and adapt as you see fit. Two- to four-year-olds can stack books, put toys away, toss laundry in the hamper, and weed-whack the yard. Five- and six-year-olds can make their beds, clear some of the table, sweep under it, and regrout the tile floor. Six- and seven-year-olds can sort laundry, put theirs away, set the table, dust, and drive the family van to the car wash. Eight- and nine-year-olds can load and unload the dishwasher, put away groceries, scrub toilets, vacuum or mop the floor, and file your taxes. Older kids can do all this and more, like reshingle the roof and field dress a deer.

Convincing your children of the virtue of housework, however, is another matter. That's when creativity comes in handy. I overheard one daughter say, "We have to get all the toys in the box before the flood comes." Nothing motivates like the threat of water damage. And if their toys are animals, you can work in a Noah theme. Productive *and* educational.

When your kids are young, novelty goes a long way. If you can creatively give them a task to do, they may delight in doing it without even realizing the chore-ness of the project. Here are some ways to get the job done without whining or complaining (from your children too): Launch the requested task into their room on a paper airplane. If you're artistically challenged, crumple the paper and pretend it's a hand grenade. The note you've written on it could be, "It looks like a bomb went off in here. Time to clean your room." If your child is preliterate, he may bring the paper to you unfolded and ask what it says.

You could also slide a note under the door like a secret message. If you feel like going all out, you could write it in code and give them the decoding key. Another option would be rolling up the paper like a scroll and reading it like a royal herald, "Hear ye, hear ye" and all. Or tape a speech bubble to a stuffed bear. "This room is my cave, and it's getting beary messy. That makes me wanna roar! Please help!"

Sure it's silly, but what little kid doesn't love silly? You can even use a funny voice, perhaps an accent. Friends of mine use British accents to cut the tension when having an argument with each other. Another couple sings. Try it on your kids. If they don't like being told to do things, maybe it will come easier in song. As an added bonus, if you're irritated, singing is said to help improve your mood, just like fake smiling. I might be creeping my kids out by how often I smile at them.

With her grandchildren, my mom will write down tasks as well as fun activities (but mostly tasks) on small pieces of paper and put them in a hat. The kids take turns pulling out a piece of paper and doing what it says: pick five things off your bedroom floor and put them away, fold ten pieces of laundry, etc. This method hasn't failed her yet. The kids have so much fun reading and doing the tasks, they seem to not realize they're actually doing chores. Note: this does not work on spouses!

Some children do better with specific tasks rather than a general command of "clean up your room." So, first try, "Pick up all the clothes and put them away." When they come back and the task is completed, say, "Great job. Now get all the stuffed animals off the floor." Next, "Put away the free weights. Start with the hundred pounders and work your way up." With any luck, they'll cheerfully ask, "What next, Momma?" Or they may balk and groan, dropping their shoulders to their knees. At that point you have a few options. One is to seem like the benevolent parent and offer them five more minutes of play time with the Legos, which you planned to allow anyway. Now you're viewed as the nicest parent ever. If they still complain, you can say, "Or no extra time, and you put them all away now." Whining ensues. "Do you want the extra time? Yes? I'm setting my clock for five minutes." Hopefully that will send them scurrying, knowing times a-wastin'. And if not, you bring out The Box and say, "You have until X:00 to clean your room. Everything that's still on the floor will go in the box and stay there for [one day, two days, a week — whatever you feel your child can handle]."

Of course, positive incentives for completing tasks can work, too. The girls know the general living areas need to be picked up each night. If they miss anything, I place it on the chair by the hallway leading to the bedrooms. They call it the magical chair because when I put items on it, they disappear. At story time I say, "No book until you empty the magical chair." The girls scatter, returning items to their bedrooms. Then I try not to look too closely at their rooms.

My girls are into Pokémon cards. A neighbor who introduced them to Pokémon seems to have forever changed the course of their lives. Now they spend hours playing Pokémon War and a whole slew of other games they've made up. The cards have even proven educational, as the girls have pulled out the tape measure to see how long each creature is according to the stats on the card. They've also added up all the respective "hit points" on each card into the thousands. One daughter even created a bar graph — for fun! — to demonstrate how many of each "class" of Pokémon she has. She may have been switched at birth.

In order to earn more Pokémon cards, the girls can do special tasks around the house beyond their normal chores. My husband even took them to the store to pick out a new pack, and once purchased, let them see what treasures lay within. They practically drooled over the shiny new cards, deciding which ones they wanted, and quickly asked what they could do to earn them. Soon weeds were getting pulled, baseboards were being dusted, the grizzly bear's fur was being brushed and adorned with pink ribbons. And most importantly, fewer tasks needed to be completed by Mom or Dad. That's totally worth the four dollars at Walmart.

Pokémon cards are also helpful for negative incentives. (I just made this term up. It's a euphemism for threats, but not in a horrible way, so it's still totally kosher.) My younger two girls complain about cleaning themselves (e.g., taking a bath). The funny thing is, once they're in the tub, trying to get them out is like walking past a free ice cream sample and not partaking. They can play in there for an hour, and still not begin to wash themselves. That's when the kitchen timer comes in handy. I tell them if they're not out and sparkling clean by the time it goes off, they lose a Pokémon card. Perish the thought!

Having a well-loved father is a bonus incentive for cleaning up. When my husband is on the way home from work, I tell the kids, "Let's clean up so the house looks nice for Daddy!" Not only does the house get cleaned, but their respect for their father grows, also. And did I mention the house gets cleaned?

A friend said that she and the kids spent an afternoon cleaning up as a surprise for her husband. She asked her son if he thought Dad would notice. The boy said he'd probably be so surprised he'd have a heart attack. My friend said, "Well, that'd be good," to which her son replied, "Good?! That would be terrible!" She said, "I mean, at least that way we'd know he really appreciated it." Later she reported her husband survived the initial shock, adding: "That man is *so* ungrateful."

The transformation from a pig sty to a model home is easier if you instill the one-room rule. The one-room rule is when the kids can only play and make a mess in one room at a time. When they're done playing with their taxidermy kit, they have to put it away before the Fort Knox blueprints come out. Yeah, I know. Good luck with that.

At this point, there's something to be said for limiting the number of toys in the house altogether. (Perhaps each child can choose one to give to charity.) Having fewer toys not only makes cleanup easier, it also forces kids to get creative. They might play with one item the normal way and then come up with new games for it. For instance, they can first dress their princess dolls and braid their hair, and later use them for skeet shooting practice.

Rotating out toys by putting some away for several weeks or months keeps playtime fresh. I've also heard of parents not putting the batteries in noise-maker toys until their children get tired of playing with them. Then, when it suddenly lights up or plays songs, voilà, brand new toy. I love sneaky parents like that.

You can be sneakier still, like my mother-in-law who would wrap up old toys and give them to her young children again as Christmas or birthday gifts. Until they started to notice. My husband tells me that when he was six or so, he finally caught on. After his initial excitement, he said, "Wait, I already have this!" But while the ploy lasted, gift giving and money saving were so much easier for his parents!

On the whole, in the journey toward a clean home and happy parents, get creative so the effort isn't an overwhelming chore for your kids or you. With repeated effort, your children will clean up after themselves as a matter of routine, without you having to say a word, or nearly sending your husband into cardiac arrest.

CHAPTER SEVEN

Teenagers

"Words which do not give the light of Christ
increase the darkness."

• SAINT TERESA OF CALCUTTA •

A s C. S. Lewis said in the dedication to his goddaughter in *The Lion, the Witch, and the Wardrobe,* children grow faster than books. So true. My oldest was twelve when I started this book but is now thirteen. My husband was on the other side of the country the day she became a teenager, and for several days after. Coincidence? I think not.

Knowing I'll have at least one teenage girl in my home for ten years, with two of those years filled with three teenage girls at once, scares me. I'm pretty sure this will cover my Purgatory time, taking me straight up when I die. So, there's that.

Before I had children of my own, I worked one summer with a mother of teenagers. She called home around 10:00 a.m., and when her teenage kid answered the phone, she said, "Oh, I'm sorry. Did I wake you?" And get this — she wasn't being sarcastic. She continued, "Well, there are a few things that need to be accomplished today. Do you have a piece of paper and something to write with?" She then listed the tasks she wanted her kids to complete while she was at work. There were no signs of backtalk coming from the other end of the line, nor did this mom need to repeat herself or take a stern tone. This, I thought, is an impressive woman.

This respect between mother and children was mutual. For one thing, she remembered that one of the greatest joys of summer vacation was the ability to sleep in. She didn't chide their laziness, but apologized for disrupting them. One would think this is a sign of a pushover parent, yet the fact that they took notes for their chore list would suggest something far more powerful at work here: Magic! Or more realistically, teenagers who love their mom because she understands them.

Your normal garden-variety teenager doesn't like being told what to do. This mom instead let her kids know what "needed to be accomplished." She gave them latitude on when it needed to be completed: before she got home. Teens like to feel they are in control. If you want your son to take out the trash, you'll have better luck saying, "The trash needs to be taken out before dinner," than, "Take the trash out now." Yes, you're the parent, but your teen feels less like a kid when he still gets some say in the matter, even if just the timing. But, of course, if he wants to eat dinner, he'll have to take the trash out first. I wouldn't suggest telling him to do it before bedtime, or he may just pull an all-nighter.

Another way to protect a teen's beloved autonomy and save yourself some trouble is to guide them toward problem-solving on their own. For example, the last twenty minutes before the younger girls' bedtime is book time. Once, when I announced book time, my oldest started crying because she's at that age where every little thing sets her off, and because she had planned to play a game with her sisters. She was upset there wasn't enough time now. I asked if she preferred the game over listening to *The Fellowship of the Ring*. Then I sat back and watched her work it out: "I was looking forward to playing the game all day. Finishing my history homework took too long. There isn't time for the game now." And finally, "I guess we might as well read." Good choice, and she stopped crying because she had made the decision on her own. That was preferable to me telling her what was going to happen, whether she liked it or not.

That was an easy one. Sometimes, teenagers require more massaging from the parent, such as suggesting possible solutions and guiding them toward the best conclusion. Asking, "What do you think you should do?" is a good default question. And if that doesn't work, put your foot down like my grandparents had to do with my mom. The story goes that her dad tried (and failed) to help her with her algebra. He finally said, "If you can't do this, you might as well stay home and help your mother around the house because you'll never get an education or a good job." The next morning, she got up, packed lunches for her brothers, and made breakfast for everyone, having no intention of going to school ever again. That's when her parents stepped in and said, "Uh, no. But thank you for the eggs. We like them burnt."

As the parent, you already know what your kid should do, but it's okay to act dumb. In fact, sometimes that's the better option. Take the example of my friend Jenny. When she was a teenager, her church searched for people to form a band to help celebrate some of the Masses. Being a guitar player, Jenny was excited, until the worst possible thing happened: her mom told her she should do it. Jenny was devastated. Now she couldn't! Not after her mom's prodding.

The same announcement was made several weeks in a row, and each time Jenny was hopeful, but after every Mass her mom suggested she join, saying, "You'd be great at that!" To which Jenny could only reply to herself, "I know I would, so stop mentioning it so I can!" Finally, no doubt exasperated, her mom stopped bringing it up. Then Jenny had to wait two more weeks before joining to leave no doubt that this was her own decision.

At least Jenny's mom wasn't a helicopter parent. If she had been, she would've just signed Jenny up herself, not giving her daughter the opportunity to take charge on her own. Parents who hover end up robbing their children of the ability to learn and mature. It's like they don't want their kids to ever leave home. I don't understand.

When it comes to Jenny and the story of the church band, her mom was lucky that what Jenny wanted to do was something good. Teenagers aren't known the world over for having terrific judgment or willpower. At a retreat I attended, a priest shared a story about a teenage boy struggling with pornography. The priest's advice to him was to not put salt on his food the next day. The day after that, no ketchup. Then, not to drink any soda. The point was to slowly build up his tolerance for denying his will. If this young man could keep himself from giving in to increasingly more challenging temptations, he'd be better equipped to fight off the urge to look at porn. We can use that advice in so many areas of our lives, but impulse control is especially necessary with teens. Remind them that strong willpower will benefit them throughout their lives, like when they're tempted to read all the scholarly writings of William Shatner in one night. Such pearls of wisdom need to be spread out over time (and space) to be truly appreciated.

Saint Teresa of Calcutta saw the face of Jesus in every person she picked up from the street. We know Christ said that when we feed the hungry, give drink to the thirsty, comfort the sick, etc., we do this also to him. Start building this practice in your children by reminding them of the words of Christ every time they encounter a homeless person or someone with a physical or mental disability. Eventually learning to put the face of Christ on everyone they encounter will help them to be kind. Then, as teenagers, potentially drawn into the prevalent immoral culture, this practice will help prevent them from exploiting others for their own personal gain. "Visualize Christ's crucified face on that person. Do you still want to do that to her?"

Imitating Saint Teresa would also make it harder for your child to be a bully. Kids generally become bullies because they feel inadequate and, therefore, will overcompensate or hide that fact by lashing out at others, hoping to make themselves feel better and/or rise in the esteem of their friends. If you find out your child is bullying others, get to the root of the situation. Ask him what's going on that he feels justified in behaving that way. Brainstorm how he can feel better about himself, perhaps by getting involved in something constructive like basketball, drama, band, or submarinebuilding. If it turns out your kid is just mean, my condolences. Ask why he's being so uncool. When he can't come up with a good excuse — because there is none — ask what reason he has to continue his behavior. Besides, has he watched movies? Nobody cheers for the bully, but they do applaud when he gets what he deserves in the end.

If your child is the one getting bullied, remind him that bullies love to get a reaction, so don't give him the satisfaction. Show a lack of concern by making a joke.

Bully: "Hey, Camel. Nice nose."

Kid with big nose: "Thanks. If anyone wants to know what's for lunch today, just ask me. I can sniff the cafeteria from here!"

He can end the conversation with, "Hey, smell ya later!" Perhaps you can help your child come up with snappy comebacks, but not ones that could insult the bully, like, "I could smell you coming a mile away." Antagonizing a bully is never a good idea. But if your child shows he can't be moved by harassment, the bully will often search for a new victim.

Another issue of this age group is peer pressure to do the usual bad things: drink, smoke, shoplift, hook up, cut class, and spray paint "Call your mom and tell her you love her" on the sides of buildings. Since this generally comes from classmates, and my kids are homeschooled, they have to pressure each other.

"Hey," one whispers, "let's finish our work quickly so we can play."

"I don't know. It sounds risky. What if we get caught?" Plus, there's no way for them to skip school without me knowing about it. They have such a deprived childhood.

If you get wind of your teen being pressured by his peers, here are some ideas. First of all, you can't rely solely on "Don't do it because I said so," or "It's bad," or even, "God disapproves." Teenagers are old enough to understand reality and consequences, so explain exactly why these activities are harmful, physically and spiritually, and what can happen if they partake. A strong foundation of knowledge will keep them from caving. Also, if once upon a time you did the thing you're trying to tell your kid not to do, don't tell them that. Your credibility will be shot.

In general, a teenager's best defense against peer pressure is for the parent to have already ingrained proper values in him. Maybe they won't outright say to their friends, "This is wrong," but a "Nah, I'm good" will imply that answer. If they have the guts to be the light to their friends, that's stupendous. For this to be effective, it has to be done in a loving, understanding, nonjudgmental manner, like we parents have hopefully demonstrated. They can't just tell their friends a particular behavior is wrong. They must express worry or concern. Their friends won't like being told what to do, naturally, but they'll be more receptive if the delivery doesn't feel like an attack. Your teens could provide alternative activities that are safer physically and morally. Perhaps you can host a party at your house. Maybe a disco theme. Kids are into that these days, right? I'm totally up on what's hip and groovy.

When all else fails, your teen may need new friends. My brother, Luke, had a friend named Kyle, whom my parents knew was no good. When Kyle came to pick Luke up from the house one day, my parents made Luke tell Kyle they couldn't hang out anymore. That was probably the hardest thing my brother had ever done. But thank God he did it. And Luke was probably, on some level, grateful for the intervention.

It may not be that easy to get your child away from a bad influence. The best bet may be to find him a new group of friends. Try sports. If the bad influences are on his team, then a different sport. Ideally, all those games and practices will keep him too busy to get into trouble.

Another option could be horseback riding if there are stables nearby. Young women rescued from human trafficking frequently go back to that lifestyle because it's all they know. Horseback riding has been found to be an effective mechanism to change their behavior. In their new setting, they also learn to feed and groom a particular horse. They become so attached to the animal, they don't want to leave it, and therefore, don't go back to their traffickers. If you have a child influenced negatively by his or her friends, and a sport isn't going to cut it, try getting him or her involved with horses. And if not horses, a puppy, ferret, or capybara — something your teen can be responsible for and love. On that thought, maybe nix the ferret.

Sports can keep your teen out of trouble, but an unfortunate side effect of athletics is the possibility of pride and boasting about how many free throws he can make into the goal for the two-point conversion in three strokes under par. Everyone has been given a unique set of skills and abilities, athletic or otherwise. Remind your kids that these are gifts from God, and we should honor him for them, not ourselves. Therefore, sports or other activities can also provide a means for practicing humility. In our social media age, keeping quiet about accomplishments can be a challenge. Get your children in the habit of asking themselves and answering truthfully about their motivation for posting something on Instagram, Twitter, etc. For example: I want to post this picture of myself snowboarding online. Why? Is it because I want a job as an instructor, and I need to show them I have the chops for it? Is it to show people what I'm interested in so they get to know me better? Or, is it to showoff how cool I am? If I'm motivated by pride, I shouldn't post it. Train your kids to question their motives and be honest with the answer.

Since teenagers need guidance when it comes to humility (unlike babies, who are born humble; you pat them on the back and they just fall asleep) making the Litany of Humility part of the daily routine will help. At the school where my husband works, a section of the Litany is recited each morning as part of the schoolwide announcements, with the full prayer completed by the end of each week. As a result, the students are humbled by regularly tripping over their feet, falling down stairs, running into lockers, and asking girls who are way out of their league out on dates. I'm kidding, of course, but I have heard people say that humiliating things happen to them after praying the litany.

I haven't had that experience. Maybe God thinks nothing special has to happen for me to achieve the same effect: "She allows herself to be seen in public. That ought to do it."

Handing a copy to your teen and saying, "Pray this," may not go over well. Subtlety would be wise in these murky waters, like taping a copy to the bathroom mirror — yours as well. Then when asked, you can say, truthfully, that we all need to work on humility, and that saying the prayer while brushing your teeth saves time while simultaneously promoting proper hygiene. Don't spit until you reach the Amen.

Humility can easily be confused with humiliation, though. Since teenagers are embarrassed easily, believing all eyes are on them all the time, it's helpful to have some phrases at the ready to get them through. My dad knew better than to tell me, as a teenage girl, that I was overreacting. However, he sometimes did gain traction with that immortal phrase, "Don't sweat the small stuff." Since I am, ahem, much older now, it's easy to recognize how pointless so much was back then. At the time it was another story. But in the grand scheme of life, wearing the same dress as another girl on the same day is no big deal. (As an adult, not only did I wear the same dress as another to a wedding, we sat next to each other. Somewhere during the first reading, we finally noticed and got a good chuckle.) Being able to laugh at yourself is a great quality which makes a person more likeable. Plus, if you're laughing, too, everyone else can only be laughing with you, not at you.

If encouraging me to laugh it off didn't work, my mom would say to me, "Who will remember this one week from now? Two weeks from now? Or a month from now?" The answer: practically no one, besides me. Why? Because everyone else is focused on their own embarrassments and whatever new crazy thing happened in school that day. By tomorrow, it will be something different, and your thing will be old news. So, no matter how mortifying an event may be to one individual, it will blow over soon enough, forgotten, and usually replaced by some other poor schlub's misfortune.

When I'd get upset about something that couldn't be laughed away, like missing out on a trip to an amusement park with my friends, my dad would say, "It wasn't meant to be," as in, it wasn't in the capital P Plan. We may never know why something goes the way it does, but we can trust that God has his reasons, and those are the best. Perhaps when we get to heaven we can ask him, "How come I didn't get to go to Cedar Point with my friends when I was fourteen?" But then again, in case you're only granted one question for the Almighty, be sure it's a good one. Ask something you've always wanted to know, something meaningful and profound like, "So who *is* buried in Grant's tomb?"

Zooming ahead for a moment to college-aged Betsy, I still struggled with my impatience and irritation with things not going my way. I had a roommate who masterfully dealt with me in these situations. Say we were running late to something and I was hitting every red light possible, which is always the case when running late. I'd fume at every stop. She'd come up with a story as to why this had to happen, something like, "If we'd made this light, we would nearly hit a dog who, startled, would jump, landing on a woman carrying a ball of yarn which would fall and roll across the filthy sidewalk getting all dirty and ruined when she planned to use it to knit a scarf for her new grandchild. Then that poor baby would be cold this winter all because you got this light green." The more ridiculous the story, the more she'd make me smile. Try this with your impatient kids, who are easily flustered when things don't go their way.

If you have a stubborn one who persists in his "woe is me" attitude, be like my mom who would wisely remind me that no matter how bad I thought I had it, there was always someone who had it worse. You could obnoxiously recite this poem, which works well for little kids, too: "I was in the blues because I had no shoes, until I saw a man on the street who had no feet." It puts life into perspective.

"It was nice while it lasted" is another useful phrase. Sure, a good thing came to an end, like the chocolate chip cookie dough ice cream, but focusing on the blessing that was had, even for a short while, makes one happier than dwelling on the void in the freezer.

In particularly sticky situations, ask your teen this: "What is the worst thing that can possibly happen?" Use it, for example, if your kid is in anguish over the need to ace a test, or get into the college of his dreams: Wichita University of Applied Yodeling. Though, whatever they tell you may be the be-all and end-all of horribleness, gently remind them that, ultimately, the worst thing that could ever possibly happen, no matter what the situation, would be going to hell. Then ask if failing that test would result in going to hell. Of course it wouldn't. Hopefully that perspective will help them lighten up a little. Although, Wichita University of Applied Yodeling sounds like hell to me. Your kids should shoot for the rival college: Pretty Prairie College of Fly Fishing. (I mean no disrespect to readers from Kansas. There's no place like home.)

If, despite your best efforts, you have a teen who wants to argue with you over something unimportant like who would win in a cage fight, Malibu Barbie or a My Little Pony (Twilight Sparkle all the way!), my advice is to not bother. Keep your mouth shut or say only the minimum necessary to end the conversation. It's not worth it. Your child will not let you win. You'll both be in a worse mood, and have wasted time and energy. Even when he or she is wrong, let it go. Smile and move on. You'll be in a happier, healthier mental place if you don't go down that unending road.

Here's where the quote from Saint Teresa of Calcutta at the beginning of this chapter comes in: "Words which do not give the light of Christ increase the darkness." If what you want to say won't help the situation, don't say it. How great it would be if your teen followed this advice, too. That quote might be worthy of a central place on the fridge.

I remember getting scared when my brother, seven years older than I am, would have yelling matches with my dad over nothing. Scarier still was about seven years later when I became a teenager myself, and likewise had shouting matches with Dad.

How much easier it is to yell rather than striving to remain calm. And, though I have yet to test this principle, I can't help but think that if my dad hadn't shouted back, maybe I would've stopped yelling, too. It's far less satisfying to raise your voice to the highest decibels when the person you're aiming for is responding in a normal tone. Not that I blame my dad for not trying this. No doubt I deserved the full weight of his vocal cords, but I can't help but wonder if I would've kept up my tirade if he weren't, essentially, feeding my anger by responding in kind.

I know parents who have hung punching bags in their teenager's room to help them relieve frustrations. This could be worth a try. If nothing else, maybe your teen will get buff. That'll be useful when you want the groceries carried in: "Look, Mom, one trip!"

Once, my mom knocked on the bathroom door, asking me to hurry up. I flung it wide, banging it against the wall, and screamed, "Just leave me alone!" and ran crying to my room. I can still picture my brother, watching TV in the living room, leaning his chair back to gawk.

Not my finest moment.

Mom followed me upstairs, sat on the edge of the bed, and said, "Okay, what's going on?" I then launched into all the things that were bothering me, big and small. Among them: the local ice cream parlor going out of business despite my frequent patronage, I got a hole in my favorite jeans (they really were the best; RIP, my denim friend), and my parents wouldn't let me attend a youth group because they said it was too far away. (Mom relented after seeing how important it was to me.) As I gushed forth my grievances against the universe, she sat there, calmly and patiently, until I was done. I felt much better afterward. All I needed was for someone to listen.

When your kids blow a gasket, maybe a sympathetic ear is all that's required. Or, they might honestly want you to leave them alone. It's hard to tell with teenagers. A good rule of thumb is to ask what's wrong, and if you're told, great. Hold back on giving advice unless you're asked. And if they don't want to talk about it, you can let them know you're around if needed.

If you follow the suggestions in the next chapter you'll have an easier time guarding your teenager's heart and soul. Raising one right means having less to worry about. Above all else, show your kids you love them so that they'll feel more comfortable coming to you with their struggles. And never forget to pray for them, tossing in the occasional sacrifice for good measure. That same mom who called home to give her teenagers their chores for the day, told me another time she offered a major struggle up for her son. When she returned from work, she found him to be the happiest, most pleasant self he'd been in some time. Knowing the power of suffering is an incredible gift of our faith.

One final story. My mom was a high school freshman in Virginia when desegregation happened. A lone African American girl named Carol appeared in her English class. Carol was shunned and picked on mercilessly. Since Carol had no friends, my mom befriended her. This meant that my mom was then made fun of, called an n-word lover, etc. Even when oranges and apples were thrown at them in the cafeteria, she continued to be Carol's friend, though they took their lunches elsewhere from then on. Years later, my mom was invited to Carol's wedding.

There's such a thing as the bystander effect, where, so long as other people are around, no one will take action in an emergency, hoping someone else will. If you teach your teenagers to be compassionate and holy, they'll be the one person who steps up. After all, the saints were often the ones who did.

CHAPTER EIGHT

Keeping the Faith

"If you do not live what you believe, you will end up believing what you live."

• VENERABLE FULTON SHEEN •

There's one in every family, right? The child who doesn't keep the Catholic faith. Perhaps a liberal college was his downfall. Maybe he started running with a bad crowd. Whatever the cause, a child who loses the faith is an incredible strain on a faithful parent. Just look at Saint Monica. Did you know that her son, Saint Augustine, once took off on a boat, leaving her standing on the dock because he was tired of her tagging along with him everywhere? When I read that, I was like, "Dude, that's harsh." She, of course, never gave up on him, for which he was grateful, eventually. If that happened to the rest of us, we'd probably throw our hands up, say "Whatever," and reach for the nearest corkscrew.

Saint Monica is our example and patroness for wayward children. Her continual prayer brought her son around. Praying daily for our kids is the first step toward success with keeping our kids Catholic. Why not go for broke and pray for them to become saints? Saint Zélie Martin, mother of Saint Thérèse of

Lisieux, and Marie Vianney, Saint John Vianney's mom, dedicated their children to God at birth or before, and their children became saints. I'm not saying that doing so is guaranteed to get your child canonized, of course, but it certainly helps. Zélie Martin used this prayer: *"Lord, grant me the grace that this child may be consecrated to you, and that nothing may tarnish the purity of its soul."* So short and simple, yet powerful.

Marie Vianney taught her children about Jesus and Mary when they were babies. I'm trying to do the same with baby Joe. Maybe he'll become super holy and his first word will be "Jesus." Or, "transubstantiation." So, every time I carry Joe out of my bedroom, I point out the crucifix and say, "Jesus. This is Jesus." But Joe ignores me, grabs the cross, and scrapes it back and forth across the wall, leaving a mark in the paint. Someday years from now when we're moving, I'll take the cross down, see those scratch marks and think, "Awww … That's going to bring down our resale value."

When your children are a little older, they can participate in a family rosary. Until then, they can at least be present to start hearing and learning the prayers. My sister-in-law said that during their family rosary, her one-year-old was playing with her mother's phone, and during a Hail Mary they were interrupted by Siri's voice informing them, "I'm sorry, but Mary, Mother of God, is not in your contacts." My sister-in-law was grateful that her children were enunciating well enough for Siri to make this mistake, but also sad Jesus' mother wasn't in her contact list. Shouldn't she be in all our contact lists? Another little boy I know, when asked who his mom is, says, "I have two: my mom and Jesus' mom." Right on, kid. Right on.

Family prayer provides an opportunity to invite your children to add their own petitions. It's a great way to find out what's on their mind. You'll also have a heads up when they don't get an answer they were wanting. Here's your chance to teach them that God answers our prayers in one of three ways: yes, no, or wait. God says no to our prayers when our request isn't good for us. When he says yes, we asked for the right thing. If the response is "wait," then it's just not the right time. If they're persistent, maybe their prayers will be answered and the New England Patriots finally *won't* make it to the Super Bowl.

Another way to get your kids in the prayer habit, beyond family prayer, is teaching them the morning offering. You can point out that by praying it, they're dedicating their day to God by offering him their work. This means that whatever tasks they complete, they're doing not just for themselves or for you, the parent, but for Jesus. Is it right to offer anything less than our best to God? Of course not. Therefore, we should do our utmost in everything: schoolwork, chores, being kind to our siblings, not shaving Daddy's mustache while he's sleeping, etc. Saying, "God is watching" is creepy, but saying, "God knows what you're doing, so let's be sure he'll be pleased with it" is a little better. "Let's always give God our best," is, well, the best.

Here's a morning offering I use. If it works for you and your kids, have at it:

O Jesus, through the Immaculate Heart of Mary, I offer you my prayers, works, joys, and sufferings of this day, in union with the holy sacrifice of the Mass throughout the world, in reparation for my sins, for the holy souls in purgatory, for sinners everywhere, sinners in the universal Church, those in my home, and within my family. Amen.

You could also suggest to your children that they simply wake up and say, "How should I spend this day? What do you want me to accomplish, Lord?" When I prayed that this morning, what came into my head was, "Write that in your book." And, done! I've completed my goal. Pass the ice cream. Then, throughout the day, whenever they think of it, your children could say something like, "Jesus, I love you. I give my life to you. I give my all to you. Please take all that I am." Just the thought of Jesus, here and there, ought to help keep your kids on the right path.

The guardian angel prayer is another good one that comes

in handy when faced with an uncomfortable situation. Praying to your guardian angel to ask the other person's guardian angel to soften that person's mind and heart will help that confrontation go more smoothly.

Now that you've taught your children an arsenal of prayers to say, they'll need to learn from your example what not to say. We must be careful with this — small ears pick up everything. Have you heard the joke about the priest who came to dinner, and the young child used a swear word in front of him? The parents said, "I don't know where he learned that. He never leaves the house!"

In addition to unsavory word choice, we must avoid speaking poorly of others or gossiping. One friend calls gossip "porn for women." It sets a bad example, is sinful, and is so easy to find some justification for. "I just need to be well-informed." Mhmm. Help your children, and yourself, be happier by not having minds cluttered with information that doesn't belong there.

There's an Arab proverb that says: "The mouth should have three gatekeepers: Is it true? Is it kind? Is it necessary?" I discovered the truth of this in the car when my husband was driving at the wheel and me from the backseat. I was close to correcting his driving, as was my duty in that position, when it occurred to me that maybe I didn't have to say anything. It wouldn't do any good anyway. Then I wondered if there are other times where I could survive not expressing what I was thinking and not letting others marvel at the wonder of my thoughts. Lo and behold, there were! For example, I didn't need to provide a response to everything that was said around the dinner table, even if I disagreed. In fact, speaking less made the chaotic dinner table (I have three girls, remember) slightly less like jabbering monkeys on parade. Less noise meant more peace, and that makes me happier. It may even make my kids happier too. Mind blown!

It might be harder to convince your children to talk less, but eventually they may catch on. Remind them that it's so easy to sin through our words, so to be on the safe side, if it doesn't need to be said, don't say it. It's like the sequel to "If you don't have anything nice to say, don't say anything at all." If you don't have anything helpful or necessary to say, you don't need to say that either.

A local priest is fond of the expression K.Y.M.S., which stands for Keep Your Mouth Shut. Or, possibly Kangaroos Yell at Miniature Squash. I forget which. This priest recognizes that so much discord in family life (and elsewhere) stems from people saying things they shouldn't, or continuing to squabble over something minor when they should just let it go. Teach your kids: if it doesn't pass that Arab proverb test, just zip it. Spare those around you from hurt or bad feelings that will be difficult to reconcile. The brain has a harder time forgetting negative experiences than it does positive. Encourage your children to fill the home with uplifting words only. (Yet another reason I insist my whine-inclined daughter do her griping in the privacy of her own room. The rest of us don't need to be brought down by her.)

Admittedly, getting children to mind what they say is an uphill battle. Reminding them over and over to guard their tongue can be exhausting. Maybe your family would benefit from K.Y.M.S. written on the fridge with magnets. That would be a more pleasant reminder than what a friend mysteriously found left on her fridge by a pre-literate child: the letters d, i, e, and t — in that order!

Training your children to watch what they say requires perseverance, on your part, and on theirs. This is a great virtue worth ingraining in kids. My friend's children wanted to give up while putting together a 1,000-piece puzzle. She encouraged them to keep going, saying, "Think how good it will feel when you put the last piece in!" Of course, as it turned out, three pieces were missing. Still, they had persevered to that point!

Such instances can help your children obtain another great skill and virtue: detachment. An elderly friend I used to visit with my young children was fond of small angel figurines. She had approximately one million throughout her small house. Naturally, this made for a nerve-racking experience, as my children wanted to handle them, all of them. It was less of a visit with her and more of a constant taking-objects-from-my-children-and-putting-them-back-where-they-belonged sort of thing, but she loved seeing the kids. The best part was ... well, no, the best part was that not a single object broke, miraculously; but other than that, the best part was her continually saying, "It's okay if one breaks. They're just objects." Her detachment was remarkable. That was a great lesson for young kids (mine) and, ahem, older kids (me): things are merely that — things. When I learned Saint Teresa of Calcutta died owning nothing but her rosary beads and the clothes on her back, I was inspired. Stuff is not what's important in life. Our love for God and each other is what is truly important. Opportunities to teach this abound. The peace of realizing this for ourselves makes for a happier us, too.

Learning detachment also makes the all-important virtue of charity easier. If your church has a food pantry, let your children pick out something from the store (or your cupboard) to contribute. At Christmas time, when the Toys for Tots boxes appear, maybe your kids would like to buy a toy for children less fortunate. When it comes to spending their own money, you can help them learn about tithing while they're young. I recommend giving them three envelopes or three red plastic cups like you use for margaritas at parties, and labeling them: Spend, Save, Give. You can determine the percentages that go into each. Establishing this habit early will likely help them budget as well as tithe later in life, instilling the reminder that we owe all to God.

Children can also practice charity with one another. A mom saw her sons fighting over the last two cookies because one cookie was larger than the other. She decided to intervene, saying, "You know, Jesus would want one of you to make a sacrifice by offering the larger cookie to the other. If Jesus were here, that's what he would do." The older boy put his hand on his younger brother's shoulder and said, "You can be Jesus today."

When your children are charitable, you can further foster this and other virtues by praising their good behavior in a way that recognizes quality of character. "That was kind and charitable of you to help those who need these things more than we do.

That makes Jesus happy!" In more day-to-day instances, you can use phrases like, "You're very helpful" or "You're a nice person." These are more effective than, "That was helpful" or "That was nice." The earlier phrases help your children feel that generosity, kindness, compassion, obedience, etc., are a part of who they are. Once they internalize these qualities, they'll consistently behave in that way, allowing it to come naturally. This lays the foundation of good moral habits.

If you're concerned that your own stellar example of sanctity and goodness isn't enough for your kids, let the saints pick up your slack. Reading to or telling your children stories about the saints will provide loads of examples of good habits and living right. When your kids are older, give them saint books to read themselves. They can find their own personal way to relate and become friends with that saint, not to mention the benefit of being inspired by a human being who attained such heights of holiness. Aside from their parents, of course.

These stories of saints inspire our children to not only grow in virtue, but also to stamp out vice. When someone praised Saint Thérèse of Lisieux for her looks, her father asked the person to please stop. He didn't want Thérèse to get a big head. One of Maria von Trapp's children, I'll just pick on poor Agathe again, had grown vain about her hair. To combat this subtly, Maria spoke to another of the girls when she knew Agatha would overhear her. "It's too bad Agathe is so homely," Maria said. "The rest of you are so pretty, but she can't keep up with your looks, especially because of her hair." Agathe ran to Maria sobbing her apologies for thinking too highly of herself.

In addition to stories of the saints, you can teach your children more about their faith and how to lead a virtuous life through religious education. (We use the Faith and Life series.) One of my daughter's study questions was, "Why was Jesus poor?" She took a stab at it: "So he could live the way we do?" It was funny, but if only it were true in that we lived more like him. According to a vision of Venerable Mother Mary of Agreda, Our Lady said there is no greater gift we can offer the Lord than voluntary poverty. How wonderful it would be to have wealth but for your children not to know it. Living modestly and giving the excess to charity would be an incredible lesson once your children are old enough to catch on.

Our parish priest grew up in a modest home, and his parents drove somewhat run-down vehicles. He and his siblings weren't simply given what they wanted. They were taught to do without or to earn it themselves. This helped them appreciate what possessions they did have and not take these gifts for granted. He had no idea they were actually well-off until he was older. And did I mention he became a priest?

Guiding our children toward holiness also means vigilance in what media they consume: books, music, and movies. Preview everything you can, or check them out online with a parent's guide or some other reliable source. Protecting our kids and their innocence becomes more challenging as they get older and start to pick up on more things. With teenagers, seeing something questionable, however, can be turned into an opportunity for discussion and explanation of what was wrong with that scene, for instance. I'm not saying you should watch *Breaking Bad* with them, but when they're teens, they're going to have to slowly be made aware of the ways of the world. While they're still under your care is preferable so they can ask you questions. You'll want the truth to come from you rather than bad information from someone else.

There are many methods by which we can help our children grow in and keep the faith. One chapter is by no means sufficient to learn everything, but hopefully this short read has provided some basics to lay a strong foundation. To sum up, help your kids stick with the amazingness that is our faith through prayer, letting them befriend the saints, and finding opportunities to instruct in virtue and stamp out vice. And of course, teach them to love the Mass. If only you could get them to sit still first.

CHAPTER NINE

Children at Church

"A married woman must often leave God at the altar to find him in her household care."

• SAINT FRANCES OF ROME •

I take comfort in the above quote because, even when in the presence of God at the altar, I'm doing household care, that is, trying to keep my children quiet. It's hard to pay attention at Mass when you're wondering when you should take over holding the youngest to give your spouse a break. Or, you're spending your prayers wishing the priest would wrap it up before the baby completely breaks down. ("How long is this homily going to last?")

Parents use different methods to make it through Mass in relative peace for themselves and those around them. Some take turns going, leaving the small ones at home. That sounds lovely, but when the children are deemed old enough to attend, they might rebel against suddenly having to dress nicely and sit quietly for an hour as opposed to running free at home in their pajamas.

When taking the little ones with you, there are many approaches parents can take. In order to find them all, and their pros and cons, I did an exhaustive search for the best, most so-phisticated research from across the globe on the eternal ques-tion of how to wrangle children at Mass. In other words, I asked my friends on Facebook.

First up are parents who ascribe to the practice-makes-perfect mind-set: the more you go, the better the kids will behave. Or at least, the law of averages states that the chances of their children being bad in front of the largest audience (like Sunday Mass) de-crease the more often they go to church. There could be something to that. Plus, attending daily Mass, especially when your children discover it isn't required, sets a superb example of the importance of God and the Mass in our lives. And there's no denying it's an awesome way to start your day, if you can swing it.

One friend has a son who hated going to daily Mass. So one day, rather than dealing with the struggle, she told him they were going to a birthday party. This was true, but what she failed to mention was that they were going to church first. As they walked in, he looked around at all the older men and women in the pews and cried, "This doesn't look anything like a birthday party!"

Other parents have decent luck sitting in the front row where, instead of looking at the back of heads, their children can better pay attention to what's happening on the altar. It may help, too, if Mom or Dad whisper explanations of each part of the Mass throughout. Just be sure your kids are up for this, however, or you could end up like another parent who was told by a fellow parishioner: "Please don't sit in the front row. Your kids are very distracting." Ouch.

If you do sit in the front row, you could also end up with more than the required amount of participation from your chil-dren. For instance, during the homily, the priest walked out in front of the congregation and began asking rhetorical questions: "Why did Jesus die for us? Why did he have to sacrifice his life and be nailed to the cross for the sake of our sins?" To which a friend's son loudly replied from the front row, "I have no idea!"

I'm of the camp that feels more comfortable farther back with an aisle seat for a quick getaway should things get out of hand. But again, this position works against you if you're not careful. A friend remembers fondly when her little brother got loose from the pew and made a break for the altar. Of course her mom ran after him, but what this poor mother didn't know was that one of her darling children had left an unwrapped candy bar on her car seat. The chocolate had melted onto her white slacks on the way to church. As she ran up the aisle, it's doubtful anyone missed the sight of that brown stain.

And finally, you might think sitting in the back row is safe. However, with children you're never safe. One mom was sitting in the last pew nursing the baby. When one of her nursing pads became full, she replaced it with a new one and set the old one on the seat next to her. Before she could stop him, her five-year-old son grabbed the soggy white circle, stuck it on the top of his head, and ran up the aisle yelling, "I'm the pope! I'm the pope!"

Which brings us to the cry room, where you don't have to concentrate quite as much on keeping your children quiet. Here there is no quiet, though not all cry rooms are created equal. Some are tolerable, but in others, it doesn't feel like you're in Mass at all, especially when children *and* parents speak at full volume. Worse still is when it's treated like a playground. One mom said to the father of children who were running around, "I can't hear the priest." The man responded coolly, "Then sit in the main room." There was also the woman who not only pulled out Cheerios for her child, she then produced a bowl. And a spoon. And poured milk.

There are better ways to keep your kids happy, occupied, and quiet. Some churches have "busy bags" that can be picked up on the way in. They contain lacing cards, coloring pages, and other activities. Some moms swear by stickers and paper, even if a parent's arms, legs, and clothes are used more often than the paper. Finger puppets also seem to be popular, especially when they're fabric, so if they fall off your hand, it's a silent fall.

You can't go wrong with books, especially if they're about saints or the Mass, like the ones by Fr. Lawrence Lovasik (*My Picture Missal, Picture Book of Saints, Good Saint Joseph, Mary our Mother, The Miracles of Jesus, The Angels,* etc.), or an age-appropriate Baltimore Catechism. If the book provides pictures and explanations of the different parts of the Mass, you can help your child turn the pages to keep up and follow along.

I used to hand my youngest daughter a missalette and tell her to find page number 216, or count how many pictures are on the pages, or find a word that starts with A, etc. These had the double benefit of helping her practice her number and letter skills. Parenting win!

Some parents are adamant about no food or toys in church. Instead, they set clear behavioral expectations, even making a poster labeled "Mass Rules!" (nice pun) and going over them beforehand. One family has their children practice by sitting silently with them on the couch!

Another option is setting goals and charting progress, with small rewards for individual successes (what child doesn't love getting to light one of those little votive candles?) and bigger rewards for a track record of success, like good behavior for a month. To encourage your children to work as a team, you could also offer group rewards, such as brunch after Mass at a restaurant, staying up an extra fifteen minutes at bedtime, or a special dessert.

You could also decide on consequences for bad behavior, like going to bed five minutes early for every minute they misbehave during Mass, explaining that Mass time is far more important than other time. Just don't make saying prayers or reading the Bible a punishment. You don't want them to have a negative association with these things.

One parent quizzes her children or offers a treat for someone who tells something they learned at Mass. This motivates them to pay attention. Others send their kids out for a children's liturgy, giving themselves a breather. There's also the divide and conquer method where mom holds the youngest, and dad keeps the second youngest wrangled in his arms. And of course, any kids who quarrel with each other or get rambunctious when seated next to each other need to be separated. Consider the Mass time, too. Are your children a little more sedate at one Mass time, or another?

If you want your children to respect the Mass, the priest, and all the amazing sacraments of our Faith, be sure you're at the right parish. Not all are the same. I recommend shopping around for the most hard-core priest and church within driving distance. It may mean switching parishes and making new friends, but a more fulfilling Mass experience is worth it, especially if the new church serves doughnuts afterward. I kid. However, those dough balls of deliciousness are great motivators for children to behave. One mom told me her child nudged a sibling, indicated his properly folded hands, and whispered, "doughnut hands."

A strong faith is more likely to develop at a parish where the priest and congregation take the Mass seriously. You can get a sense of this when visiting different parishes by, of course, the priest's homily, but also by the way people dress. Are 80 percent of them wearing Sunday best, or shorts and flip-flops? Which manner of dress is more likely to put the wearer in the proper frame of mind for worshipping and receiving Jesus? Yes, it may only be clothing, but the exterior informs the interior. Besides, you should look your best for God. Remember those stories in the Bible about the wedding feast and people being thrown out for not dressing properly? Be prepared for our Lord's coming at Communion. Let the only wailing and gnashing of teeth be over missing out on the last cinnamon-powdered doughnut.

Above all, as early as possible, kids need to understand what the gift of the Mass is all about. One parent shared a beautiful story of a girl's first holy Communion. She was encouraged to talk to Jesus in prayer after having received Communion. After Mass, her mother asked about her prayers. The girl said she told Jesus she loved him, prayed for her family and friends, and when she couldn't think of anything else, recited her multiplication tables for Jesus and told him a story. Telling God everything that's on your heart and mind, regardless of the topic, is a great practice to instill in our kids.

Another is to keep the Sabbath holy. My parents taught us that this included not shopping on Sundays. I've continued this practice as an adult. One Sunday, however, I was sorely tempted to cave. I needed several things at Costco and was seriously in the mood to get that shopping done. Though it gnawed at me, I resisted. Monday came with a surprise in the mail: Costco coupons, back in the day when they still used them, even though they had never mailed me coupons before. This batch contained savings on five or six things I intended to buy. If I'd gone Sunday, I wouldn't have had these coupons and would've kicked myself for missing out. Knowing that I love bargain shopping, I'm convinced God was rewarding me and convicting me that, indeed, I shouldn't shop on Sunday. I haven't been tempted since.

We know keeping the Sabbath holy means not doing any "servile labor" on Sundays if we can avoid it. For kids, this means homework, so encourage yours to get their work done before Sunday. When Catholic apologist Scott Hahn was in college, he and a few of his friends decided to experiment with not doing any school work on Sundays. It seemed like a foolish thing to do, but they put their trust in God that they were doing the right thing, even when they normally required that day to stay on top of the workload. After doing this for a semester, the grades of every single one of them had improved. They were convinced. God was faithful to them for following his commandment. Plus, if you can all keep your Sunday free of work, it can truly be a day reserved for our Lord in the Holy Sacrifice of the Mass and for strengthening your ties as a family. Be a happier parent knowing you're doing the best you can to help your children appreciate and respect the Catholic Faith through the Mass. Then enjoy the rest of your Sunday together with a special meal, outing, games, or a family movie. Strive to make it a day your entire clan can look forward to.

CHAPTER TEN

On Intercession and Happiness

"You pray, you love — that is the happiness of man upon the earth."

• Saint Jean Marie Baptiste Vianney •

One of the first items on the parental to-do list is to give our children names. The Catholic Church recommends we name each child after a saint, so he or she will have a special patron and friend in heaven. Someone told me that when we choose saint names, it isn't really us choosing our children's patrons, it's those saints choosing our children. Nice sentiment, but one I couldn't fully get behind until I heard this story from my friend, Carol. She planned on naming her baby Anne, that is, until the moment her daughter was born. Carol took one look at the baby and said, "Her name is Emily."

Carol's traditional Catholic mother was not so keen on this change of plan. "You can't name her Emily," she told her daughter. "Stick with Anne. There's no Saint Emily."

"I'm sorry, Mom," Carol said, "I can't explain it, but I just know she's an Emily."

Carol's mom did a search through a saint book, and guess what? She found a Saint Emily. She happily showed the entry to Carol, including Saint Emily's feast day — the day baby Emily was born.

I recommend cramming your children's names with as many saints as you can, such as James Ambrose Aloysius Matthew Mark Luke John Paul II the Great Smith. We can ask these patrons to help us do a good job raising our children. I'm big on requesting saintly intercession. When we conclude family prayers, we each take a turn saying our particular saint, starting with the oldest (my husband) down to the youngest who's able to talk. Sometimes we do middle names, too, for extra points. With one child having dental issues, Saint Apollonia, patron of dentists, has earned a place in the roster. When a child is ill, we call upon Saint Gianna Molla. Since in life she was a doctor and a mother, I'm sure she understands the pain of having a sick child.

I figure since they're in heaven and therefore constantly happy, they can't be annoyed by us bugging them all the time. Apparently they don't even discriminate when we don't know which patron to ask. When my mom's friend got his boat stuck in the shallows, he dragged it out but couldn't remove the bent propeller to fix it. After spending four hours with various tools, he yelled in frustration, "Saint Anybody!" and the propeller dropped into his arms.

I even make my kids intercede on my behalf, knowing Jesus loves children so much. For instance, after grocery shopping, I put the food in the trunk and the kids in the back seat, not the other way around — learn from your mistakes — when I turned the key in the ignition and the car wouldn't start. Two more failed attempts later, I looked to my children. "Girls, please say, 'Jesus, please make the car start.'" They dutifully complied, and the car started right up. I'm tempted to believe this is entirely the work of my innocent God-fearing children, but it may also have been due to the ice cream in the trunk. God knows better than to let mint chocolate chip melt. Now, if it had been rocky road, we may have been out of luck, since we all know how God feels about the rocky road. (I hear Ben and Jerry's tried out a new flavor called "The Good Rich Soil," but it didn't test well in the focus group.)

Intercessors, big and small, are a great help, and parents need all the help we can get, from heaven or closer to home, like in the kitchen. My youngest daughter pointed this out by drawing me a picture. I recognized flowers, princesses, and heart-shaped balloons, but needed her to interpret the large swath of brown toward the bottom of the page. "Is that dirt?" I asked. She replied, "No, that's a puddle of coffee for you to drink." It made me wonder if I'd been caught licking spilled coffee off the floor.

Incidentally, I didn't become a coffee drinker until having a baby named Joe. Caffeine became essential when he was a newborn. The sleep deprivation made it all the more difficult to deal with a baby who seemed to be constantly crying and impossible to get to sleep. But when I'd think about people who truly suffer, like those in concentration camps during the Holocaust, or sent to work in Siberia, knowing that without a doubt, any one of them would gladly switch places with me, I didn't feel so bad. Who was I to complain about having to, I mean, getting to, take care of an adorable newborn? This perspective helped. Knowing everything can be offered as prayer for the poor, the hungry, the persecuted, and that our suffering isn't wasted, made me happier.

I'm happier still when I focus on the fun aspects of baby Joe, who now, months later, as I come to the end of this book, has become toddler Joe. I savor the first smile, the first laugh, the first roll, the crawling, the burping — admittedly, that one's going to come back around — the first steps, the diaper blowouts. Well, "savor" probably isn't the right word for this one, though they always made for entertaining stories for my husband. As parents, we've gotta grab our happiness from each stage, each cuteness.

I never want to forget the wide grin on Joe's face when one of his sisters is about to give him a ride across the floor in the laundry basket, slowly counting, "One ... Two ... " And him shouting, "Tee!" The same goes for when he hears a dog in the distance, springs to attention, and does his version of sign language for dog. On that last one, if you haven't gotten on the baby sign language train yet, do so. It will save both you and your child so much frustration when he can sign food, water, more, and sleep. Yes, Joe even lets me know when he's ready for a nap, which is truly amazing. Throw in the signs for please and thank you and you'll feel like the most accomplished parent ever.

Sure, kids are tough, like when one complains that he can't find his glasses, then really loses it when you tell him he doesn't wear glasses. Sometimes kids are just crazy. I don't know what your excuse is, but for mine it's hereditary. In those situations, you just need to laugh. Besides, laughing is so much more fun than crying or yelling. Plus, if you grab him and hug him saying, "Kid, you're hilarious," it will throw him off his game and maybe make him forget all about the imaginary lost glasses.

Note that these expressions of joy reflect positively on your children. When you're happy, your kids are more likely to be happy. Research shows that having an unhappy, depressed parent leads to negative outcomes for children. Is it any wonder? They learn by our example. Seeing one's parent frowning and unhappy would make any child unhappy, too. Find your happiness in the small things. For me, happiness is seeing a basket of folded laundry. Greater happiness is seeing that basket emptied.

This morning I took my own advice and decided that cleaning the bathroom mirror would be my one big cleaning task for the day. Rather than put it off, I grabbed a rag and took care of it right away with great satisfaction. I even stood back to marvel at my fabulous handiwork, feeling quite accomplished.

Later I heard laughter coming from the general direction of the bathroom. Laughing is better than crying, so I ignored it. Sometime after, that same day, I discovered water splatter marks all over my previously spotless mirror. The girls had cleaned their brother's hands and feet in the sink and merriment naturally ensued. I hung my head and sighed. My first thought was that the clean mirror was nice while it lasted, for all of two hours. I considered how I need to keep my expectations for a tidy home low. I do have children, after all. But then I realized the watermarks were a reminder that my children washed their brother themselves and while doing so, he had a blast. I left the spots, and the bathroom, with a smile.

Our vocation as parents is our path to happiness and holiness. We might think that holiness was easier for canonized saints since many of them were priests or nuns, able to dedicate so much time to prayer rather than wrangling small humans under the age of reason. But being a parent gives us an advantage. These little people provide us with so many opportunities to grow in holiness. We just need to accept the challenge, even when a pot of spaghetti sauce lands on the floor. Saints earn their halo by giving of themselves completely — pretty much the requisite for parenthood.

There are probably way more parent saints than we know of. They just never had time to write anything down for the sainthood committee. If text messages were saved, we modern parents would have a greater chance, though I'm not sure how emojis translate on the meter-o-virtue. Thankfully, we don't need to be canonized to become saints and achieve perfect happiness in heaven. We just need to fill ourselves to overflowing with love for our family. Since we attain the greatest happiness in heaven, we must get there by being holy. We become holy through love. So loving our children is the path to perfect happiness. Did you follow that last part? Feel free to reread, I'll wait.

I'm ashamed to admit that when Joe was still shiny new, a.k.a. the "fourth trimester," and I was tired and frustrated, I emailed my older sister, mother of six, to rant about how difficult motherhood is, hoping to feel better through her commiseration. (I know, right? Surely she has me beat.) She responded in one sentence: "There's nothing easy about our lot."

Her unusual word choice came back to me months later when I read this line from Saint Thérèse of Lisieux to her sister in the book *Léonie Martin*: "Our only happiness, here on earth, is to concentrate on always finding the lot that Jesus gives us delightful. And your lot, dear little sister, is a wonderful one."

And therein lies the key to happy parenting. Enjoy it!

ACKNOWLEDGMENTS

My thanks to my first readers, Flo Russell and Paul Kerekes, for their helpful feedback and for always laughing at my jokes — or at least saying they did. Also, Heather Graves, Darren Raymond, Christine Wood, and Melanie Anderson, with whom I shared snippets. I also thank so many friends and family who have shared their funny or embarrassing stories with me over the years. Too bad for you I have a good memory. My thanks to Our Sunday Visitor's acquisitions agent, Mary Beth Baker, for accepting my proposal, as well as the whole editorial team, and Rebecca Willen for being a patient, thorough, and skilled editor. Thanks to my boss and mentor, Dr. Jennifer Roback Morse of the Ruth Institute, for first making me an author. Special thanks to God (duh!), Saint Teresa of Calcutta, Saint Thérèse of Lisieux, and Léonie Martin for inspiring me with their words as I wrote this book, as well as Saint Francis de Sales, patron of Catholic authors. Thank you to my parents, because if I don't mention them, I'll be grounded. And finally, my thanks to Lisa Esquivel to whom I made the "Bluetooth baby" comment. She said, "That's funny. You should write a book." And so I have.

On Miscarriage

"Let God's grace work in your souls by accepting whatever he gives you and giving him whatever he takes from you."

• SAINT TERESA OF CALCUTTA •

A couple of times now, God has taken a look at pregnant me and thought, "I'd better keep this baby." It hurts, but it happens, and it happens to a lot of us. I know only a small percentage of mothers who haven't experienced at least one miscarriage. It helps to remember that our children are simply on loan from God. Our job is to take good care of them spiritually as well as physically before they return to him. Sometimes he asks for them back before we're ready. The difficulty is learning to surrender them to their rightful owner. If you or someone you know has had a miscarriage, and you want to know how to offer comfort, let me share with you something I was told after my first miscarriage.

Our goal, or rather, our mandate, as parents is to get our children to heaven. According to the International Theological Commission on the Vatican's website regarding "The Hope of Salvation for Infants Who Die Without Being Baptized," we can have "hope that there is a way for salvation for children who have died without baptism." And that there are "serious liturgical and theological grounds for hope that unbaptized infants who die will be saved and enjoy the beatific vision." I choose to believe that my children have arrived safely at their final destination. Therefore, instead of feeling sorry for myself, I trust those children aren't feeling sorry for themselves. How can I begrudge them the opportunity to sit on the lap of Jesus and avoid this valley of tears? When it comes to doing what I can to get my children to heaven, I'll put a check mark next to their names. Done. Mission accomplished. Those were the easy ones.

Secondly, people in heaven make great intercessors, as we know. We call upon canonized saints all the time, but everyone up there is a saint, including, we can hope, our unborn children. Now, they know no one on earth except their immediate family. Cha-ching! Work that system. Again, if we have hope that they're up there waiting for us, we might as well assume they're focusing their earthly attention on us, their family. That's why I ask for their help. I have them work for me like they're doing their chores. Praying beats taking out the garbage or emptying the dishwasher.

Parents often choose names for their children while in utero, so it's perfectly fine to give names to the children who don't make it to the outside world. I had my first miscarriage on Thanksgiving Day, which was the feast of Blessed Miguel Pro that year. I already had a relationship with Miguel on several fronts, so I saw that as a blessing, albeit a sad one to be sure. We named that child Miguelito, or little Miguel. I lost my second child on October 7, the feast of Our Lady of the Rosary. We named that child Dominic, to whom our Blessed Mother gave the mighty gift of the rosary. Whether or not they are actually boys, I have no idea. I imagine meeting them one day, God willing, and having them say, "Mom, why did you give us boy names? We're both girls!" Then I'd have to promptly rename them Michaela and Dominique. Problem solved. Good thing people up there know who we mean. I'd hate to be asking prayers of some other Miguelito and Dominic only to have them be like, "Who is this woman? Why does she keep asking us to help her find a new van?"

Although it's hard to lose a child, we can be happier parents by remembering that God loves our kids even more than we do. I trust that he would want them with him. That makes the experience of a miscarriage less difficult to bear. Ultimately, with the kids we are given, and at every age, we do the best we can and leave the rest in God's hands.

APPENDIX II

On Infertility and Impaired Fertility

It seems that every time I read the bio of a Catholic author or speaker, the first point mentioned is how many children the person has, as though this is the most important detail, giving all you really need to know about the person. That is, of course, if the person has a lot of children. Six or less kids and that tidbit is buried deep or written in size eight font.

That might seem ridiculous or paranoid if I didn't experience the small family stigma in real life. I have no doubt that many started reading this book, saw that I have four children, and thought, "Hmm ... I don't know about this lady. She doesn't seem legit."

When I still had three children, I published the article below at the website *Catholic Lane*. A friend posted it on Facebook, and the response was profound. The numbers of likes, comments, and shares were amazing. People came out of the woodwork thanking me for speaking something they thought they were alone in experiencing. Others admitted to having been judgmental (one of me personally) based on family size.

With the odds stacked against Christians of all denominations these days, and the sheer volume of issues we're collectively battling, we need to stand together. It doesn't matter how many children we have, whether they homeschool or attend private or public school, if we think using Natural Family Planning is okay, or other issues we Catholics tend to in-fight over. We're all children of God and are among the proportionally few friends he has on earth. Quarreling among ourselves is only a win for the devil. Don't fight: unite. And as you read this article below, consider loving rather than judging your fellow Catholics. We likely don't know what another couple is going through.

The Double-Edged Sword of Infertility

The pain of infertility or impaired fertility comes in more than one form. The first is the obvious suffering of the couple who wants so badly to have a child but, for whatever reason, is unable to.

Second, is the judgment of others in their Catholic community.

I've experienced this firsthand, despite having three children — an amount that's considered large by the world's standards, but "my gosh, what's wrong with you?" by Catholic standards. In the Catholic community, five children is barely skating by, six is marginally acceptable, seven or eight is a passing grade, nine to ten means you're a model Catholic, and at eleven or more you're being fitted for your halo. One's place in the Catholic hierarchy becomes dependent on the size of one's family.

So, what of the family of one or none? Even though this semi-tongue in cheek ranking is never spoken about in polite Catholic society, at least society polite enough to not do so when I'm around, Catholic couples, men and women alike, intrinsically know it and fear it, that is, if they don't measure up. They automatically qualify their family size.

One woman said, "I have one child, but we really want more." She then proceeded to explain her difficulties conceiving. Upon. The. First. Meeting.

One man said to me: "We have two, but we wanted more. We love kids!" as though I would think otherwise.

Or, modestly with a qualifier, "We have one child. We're grateful God has allowed us to have one," the second sentence speaking volumes of, "So, don't think we did this on purpose."

Why the need to explain?

Another woman told me that on the first day of Kindergarten at a Catholic school, a mom said, "Why do you only have one?" She felt compelled to tell this stranger her history of miscarriages and other fertility struggles.

I've even fallen prey to this need to explain myself to total strangers. Here's the typical situation: I'm at a Catholic mom's group, and, as is typical, there's at least a half-hour of chit-chat before we all get down to the business of the Bible study, Catholic book discussion, or Miles Christi document review. I'll exchange names with someone and the small talk inevitably leads to family size. Quite often, "How many kids do you have?" is what immediately follows, "What's your name?" Like so:

Newly-met woman: "So, how many kids do you have?"

Me: "Three," as I watch the wheels turn behind the woman's eyes as she processes this information coupled with my apparent age. I look old enough to have at least six by now. Her face softens as she gives me the benefit of the doubt, thinking I may have gotten married later in life. She tests this theory by her next craftily-worded question that will reveal all she needs to know about me.

Her: "How old are they?"

Now the jig is up. There's no hiding my apparent crime now. "11, 8, and 6." I hold my breath in anticipation of her next move as I see the corner of her eyes crinkle ever so slightly.

"Ah," she says shortly. Her smile seems a lot less natural now. If she doesn't move on to speak with someone obviously pregnant with triplets, I'm left to flounder my excuse involving an ectopic pregnancy that evidently left me handicapped in the fertility arena, not being able to get pregnant for five years now, etc. I've usually lost her by this point, as she sees someone worthier over my shoulder — a young mother of seven.

I remember a mom of half a dozen at least telling me about a mutual friend pregnant with her fourth child, all of which had been two years apart or less. "She's on track to have a nice big family," she said to me in approval.

Dear Catholic women and men of large families, we all have our struggles. For some of us, having a large family, or even any children at all, isn't in the Capital-P Plan. Please don't assume that those of us slow out of the fertility gate are doing something wrong like using NFP without serious cause, or, heaven forbid, contracepting. Please don't expect us all to be baby-making machines like the rest of you.

The day I arrived back to work from my honeymoon, a mom asked me if I was pregnant. Another mom told me her husband asked if I was pregnant. It took one miscarriage and then another year to have my first child. After which, it took a long time to get pregnant a third time. I suffered endless comments after that first child reached six months (six months!) about how she needed a friend and, "You want to have them close in age so they'll get along well."

And here I thought I'd get a reprieve once I'd finally had a child. It didn't last long. I had to explain to those who had no business knowing that my cycle took forever to return, after which point, we did indeed conceive right away, but apparently a spacing of more than two years is unacceptable.

My husband has long since stopped telling me when people at his Catholic workplace have asked if we're expecting again. I suspect that as the years have rolled by, people have long since given up asking too.

More recently, I had the misfortune of commenting how sad it made me to see my husband holding someone's infant child knowing that I wasn't able to give him another baby. A father of eight said to me, "That's on you, Betsy."

"No, it's not," I said, knowing full-well that I was doing nothing to inhibit pregnancy. He apparently begged to differ.

"That's on you, Bets," he insisted, with a bob of his head for emphasis, having worked out in his mind that I have no more children because I, and I alone, have decided it that way.

"I have literally no control in the matter," I told him.

He shook his head sadly, apparently in sorrow at the denial of my own selfishness. It was at that point that I walked away and avoided eye contact with him for the rest of the night. I managed to compartmentalize this encounter until I got home and was ready to cry, rather than have it spoil my evening out with friends.

"So this is what people apparently think of me," I told my husband. He had no answer or consoling words. He, too, understands that this is life in the Catholic bubble. I love my Catholic community, and am so grateful to have it, but, ladies and gentlemen, God does not will large families to us all. Please know that it's not possible for all of us to keep up with the rest of you model Catholic citizens. Also, note that this is not like biblical times where a women's infertility is an apparent sign of sin and disfavor from God. On the contrary, he gives each of us suffering as our path to heaven. For some that cross is more obvious to the outside world, which only adds to its weight.

So the next time you meet someone with only a few children or no children at all, who launches into her fertility history just to prove it's not her fault, please put a hand on her shoulder and say, "It's okay. I know it's rough, and I'm sorry. I'll pray for you."

You have no idea what a breath of fresh air and salve to the wound that would be for women, and their husbands, to hear.

ABOUT THE AUTHOR

BETSY KEREKES is coauthor, with Dr. Jennifer Roback Morse, of *101 Tips for Marrying the Right Person* and *101 Tips for a Happier Marriage*. Kerekes's professional experience includes journalism and public relations for Franciscan University of Steubenville. She served as proofreader and subscriptions manager for Patrick Madrid's *Envoy* magazine. She has contributed articles to *Aleteia, MercatorNet, Catholic Lane, Catholic Exchange, Catholic Mom, The Christian Post, The Southern Cross,* and *Creative Minority Report*. She has been a frequent guest on Catholic radio nationwide, was a weeklong guest on EWTN's "Women of Grace," and does public speaking. Kerekes serves as editor and director of online publications for the Ruth Institute, where she also writes weekly newsletters and manages the blog. She homeschools her children and writes about her experiences in motherhood at parentingisfunny.wordpress.com. She can be found on twitter @BetsyK1.